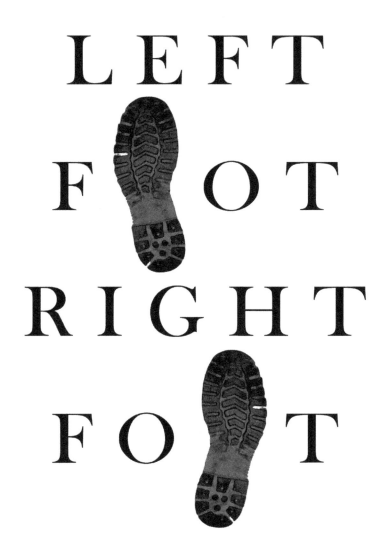

LEFT FOOT RIGHT FOOT

A Survival Guide for Business and Life

DAVID CUTLER

Left Foot Right Foot

Copyright © 2024 by David Cutler

No part of this book may be used or reproduced in any manner whatsoever without written permission, except in the case of brief quotations embodied in critical articles and reviews. For more information, e-mail all inquiries to info@mindstirmedia.com.

Published by MindStir Media, LLC
45 Lafayette Rd | Suite 181| North Hampton, NH 03862 | USA
1.800.767.0531 | www.mindstirmedia.com

Printed in the United States of America.

ISBN-13: 978-1-963844-55-9

Contents

Foreword	v
Chapter 1: Left Foot, Right Foot	1
Chapter 2: Words We Love to Hear	7
Chapter 3: Do the Opposite Day	11
Chapter 4: Perception: One of the Keys to Success	15
Chapter 5: The Skill of Observation	19
Chapter 6: Stature Is the "IT" Factor	23
Chapter 7: Gone in Sixty Seconds	29
Chapter 8: Thank You for Your Service	33
Chapter 9: Never Judge a Book by Its Cover	39
Chapter 10: The Importance of Shoes	47
Chapter 11: The Amazing Comeback	51
Chapter 12: What Is in a Name?	57
Chapter 13: Never Take Friendship for Granted	61
Chapter 14: The Most Important Meal of the Day	65
Chapter 15: Disappointment and Its Many Forms	69
Chapter 16: One Step at a Time	73
Chapter 17: The Meaning of Respect in Business and in Life	77
Chapter 18: Speak So That People Will Understand	81
Chapter 19: Humility Is Motivation	87

Chapter 20: Accomplished by 7:30 a.m. 91

Chapter 21: Music and Its Special Place in Life 95

Chapter 22: How to Recognize an Asshole 99

Chapter 23: The Gift of Color 105

Chapter 24: Power: How Do You Know Who Has It? 109

Chapter 25: Movies Are Fun, Exciting, and Relaxing 115

Chapter 26: The Podcast! 119

Chapter 27: From Beginning to the Not-So-Nice End 127

Chapter 28: Your Amazing Body and Mind 131

Chapter 29: Therapy: A Personal Relationship with Yourself 135

Chapter 30: Dear Warren Buffett 141

Chapter 31: G.O.A.T: Greatest of All Time 147

Chapter 32: The Art of Aging Gracefully 151

Chapter 33: A Lesson in Simple Adversity 157

Chapter 34: Stucco Nightmare: The Toughest
Challenge of My Career 163

Chapter 35: How Do You Eat an Elephant? 171

Chapter 36: Failure Is Winning 175

Chapter 37: One More Chapter 181

Foreword

This is a motivational book for any person's life, both in their professional world as well as their personal world. Hopefully, this book will make you smile and laugh, think and cry as you consider how the anecdotes within apply to your world. What can you do to expand and motivate yourself and others to travel through life's passages in the happiest and most productive way? We are all here for such a brief time; when we make a mistake, it is important to check ourselves and quickly regroup. We want to travel a good path, rather than be stuck in a funk for extended periods of time. When someone goes into a funk, it is difficult to think clearly and move forward. Instead, too much time is spent thinking how this happened, or why did this happen, or these people are out for me, or any excuse we can make up. Get rid of this negative energy immediately. Dust yourself off, get up, and move forward.

I often say that when you are in your thirties and forties, you can take a punch straight to the face. As you get older into your sixties and the PTSD of life sets in, you only want glancing blows—no more direct hits. It is important to plan and position yourself to be in a good place as you get older, or at least know who you are so that life's punches are only glancing blows.

Each chapter in this book is a motivational lesson that I have observed or experienced in my life. If you try and take a 30,000-foot view of your successes and failures in life, you can learn from both and hopefully will repeat the successes (and not the failures). This book speaks of so many examples of people and situations that are a view of how others motivate not only themselves, but those around them by their actions.

No one person can go through life untouched by adversity. The difference between happiness and sadness or failure and success is how you deal with adversity and rebalance yourself to survive and thrive. History is the most unutilized tool in the toolbox. Sure, there are one-time events, but most events happen repeatedly. The trick is to repeat the good things and not the bad.

In this book, I have written about the observance of life through business as well as through the real-life experiences as a person and an observer of people. I often say that people always look ahead and down; no one looks up and behind.

This book tries to give a view of all four sides of life. I hope you enjoy reading it as much as I enjoyed writing it.

CHAPTER 1
Left Foot, Right Foot

On the morning of September 15th, 2008, I woke up to the news of Lehman Brothers' monumental Wall Street investment bank collapse, starting the international banking crisis. How did this impact me, you ask? Well, here is the story from beginning to not the end.

In 1980, I started my own real estate development business. This was after graduating college and working for my uncle and father, who had both worked for their father back in the early 19th century.

After graduating from the University of Miami, my father and my uncle started a 100-lot building development in the suburbs of Philadelphia. They were purchasing the ground twenty-five lots at a time from an old farmer named Ms. Armstrong. My father and my uncle had been homebuilders for thirty-five years, as was their father before them.

We started the first twenty-five lots and built one model home that was your standard colonial home—center hall, living room on the right, dining room on the left, four bedrooms upstairs, etc. The economy was awful. After the first year, we had only sold twelve houses and were losing money with me as the only employee! It was now time to purchase the next section of twenty-five lots, and the outlook was ugly with interest rates and mortgages at an all-time high of more than fifteen percent.

Left Foot, Right Foot

My father and my uncle sat me down and told me we were going to finish the twenty-five lots over the next year and that was it. We were not going forward as things were just awful.

Down the street from our office, there were two brothers building homes. (Years later, they became the largest national homebuilder in the country, selling the "sizzle," not the steak.) Their homes were the same size as ours but had a big circular staircase, a two-story foyer, and the baths came with jacuzzi tubs. When your friend from high school walked into your new house, it screamed "Success!" These two brothers were selling the lots with these houses in a horrible economy.

I begged my father and uncle to let me build a house like the brothers down the street were doing. They argued, "We build with the best lumber, the best windows, the best insulation, and those houses are built horribly!" I said, "They are selling, and we are not, so something is catching on." They said if I could get a ground extension from the farmer, Ms. Armstrong, then they would go to the bank and try to get a loan. Ms. Armstrong was happy to help. She lived in the old farmhouse in the middle of a construction zone, so I carried her groceries in every day, walking through the mud of the construction site, and did anything else for her that she needed.

Long story short, my father and uncle went to the bank with me. We borrowed $86,000 to build a home (similar to the ones the brothers were building) on the remaining thirteen lots. This would be a "spec home." At night I went down and copied the brothers' home brick-for-brick and stick-for-stick and built it on Lot 14 in our community. It was finished in three short months (I had people working around the clock), and on opening weekend I sold twenty-six of those suckers for $30,000 less than the brothers down the street—because I had no overhead, no trucks, and no employees. I made a profit of $40,000 per home, and in one year I was a millionaire at age twenty-six.

My father and uncle turned to me after opening weekend and said, "Kid, give us $3,000 for the dump truck and trailer then pay the bank back the $400,000 for the ground and house loan. Good luck." They gave me a pat on the ass and sent me off to my one-room office about twenty minutes away.

Fast-forward twenty-eight years. We had built 12,000-plus houses throughout the Philadelphia suburbs and were facing huge headwinds due to the financial collapse in September 2008. Our main lender was Wachovia Bank, and we owed $150 million dollars in loans. One month later, October 3rd to be precise, Wachovia Bank "ran into the ditch and crashed," forcing the federal government to make a deal with Wells Fargo Bank to acquire the assets of Wachovia Bank.

I was sitting in my office and watching all the drama unfold when I received a call from Wells Fargo Bank that they had just acquired all of our loans from Wachovia. They wanted to meet to discuss how we would move forward. A meeting was set in a month at the old offices of Wachovia Bank. The night before, I laid in bed and wondered what happened to Wachovia and what was going to happen to the long-standing relationships that I had with all of my friends there for the past twenty-some years.

The next day, I entered the room and saw several of my friends from Wachovia, but the people leading the meeting were all from Wells Fargo. We started the conversation with small talk then evolved into a serious business discussion about the loan that was set to expire in the next month. Appraisals would be required on all properties. At that moment, we had fifteen communities under construction that comprised over 250 homes in one stage or another and were building about five hundred homes per year in the Philadelphia suburbs. It was clear to me through body language and tone that Wells Fargo did not want to extend my loans. And, if they did, they wanted a plan for how everything was going to get paid off in the future. They continued to refer to the fact that real estate values had plummeted; when the appraisals came back, the loan was going to be "underwater." What does that mean? Underwater means there is more debt than value. Let's say the loan started out with $250 million in real estate value and $150 million in debt. Now they are saying in broad terms that the real estate had plummeted in value due to the monetary crisis or $100 million and the debt was higher than the real estate value by $50 million.

As the appraisals trickled in, the unwelcome news became reality. The loans were greater than their values. Their values were extremely low, but the other side of the coin was that there was no one to sell it to in this market to substantiate the value or pay the bank off. The trouble soon started with all kinds of threatening mail from Wells Fargo about how all this real estate had to be collateralized with other real estate to "right size" the loan to value. In other words, the bank wanted us to pay down the loan or put up outside collateral to support this loan. This was becoming a complete nightmare with nowhere to go until real estate values returned to normal levels, which would take years. All of the builders in our industry were in the same boat. Some had options or friendlier bankers; others just threw in the towel and declared bankruptcy.

At the time, my son went to the oldest private school in the Philadelphia area. As all of the chaos was unfolding, I happened to be at the school for an event and ran into one of my son's classmate's dads. We had become friendly over the years, and I really enjoyed talking to him about business. He had a Harvard MBA and was the vice chairperson and CFO of a Fortune Fifty company—obviously a guy anyone in business would look to for advice.

That night I had a chance to speak to him privately and explained briefly how this chaos was unfolding. He was familiar with the market and understood both business and banking problems. As I watched him digest the facts, he looked at me and in a profoundly powerful voice says, "The only way to approach this is to keep your head down, put one foot in front of the other, and keep swinging. LEFT FOOT, RIGHT FOOT." I watched as he moved one foot in front of the other and kept punching in the air.

I was astonished that this was the advice from a Harvard MBA and CFO of a Fortune Fifty company. I thought I was going hear some technical, deep-routed manner from a brilliant business mind to work out my problems. Instead, I heard what the only practical solution to an impossible problem would be. No technical advice was going to fix this in a nutshell. The advice given was the advice taken—take one day at a time, do not look up, and just keep fighting through the chaos and you will get to the other side. This is the precise advice I followed, and it has gotten me through all of the problematic issues that had to be resolved over the past seven years.

This is the title to my book — Left Foot, Right Foot.Survival guide to business and life Of course, you must go to lawyers, accountants, and other experts when you are faced with banking and business issues, but the most interesting part of this experience is how there is no one to go to in these circumstances to fix things on a "global basis." Lawyers are like doctors—some operate on hearts, some do eyes, and some do bones. No doctor does it all. The same is true with lawyers; each has a specific area they specialize in. None of them that will guide you through the global chaos—you are on your own. This is why following the "Left Foot, Right Foot" advice is the true guide. You must keep moving forward through the problems and the lawyers and the experts until the answer become clear. The lawyers are good, but it is not in their best interest to make the solution happen overnight. They want the paying customer to keep paying for as long as possible. In business we strive to "fix" things right away, but law just does not work that way. Everything is slow, and it goes back and forth till it is resolved. You must push everyone like crazy to get to resolutions.

The facts are clear. When you get in trouble due to outside forces, you need to wake up every day and use the same energy you did to make money to get out of trouble. There is tremendous fog in trouble, but you need to keep you mind as clear as possible so that you can fight through the issues. It is extremely hard to get where you are, so do not give up—fight through it with the same energy to get to the other side. "Left Foot, Right Foot" is the advice I used for the balance of my business career, and it's always started me off on the right foot.

CHAPTER 2
Words We Love to Hear

Wow, what incredible words if someone can describe you as "a great dad." That is not an easy job to achieve, but it is one of the most rewarding things in life! I was married three times and have four kids (and as I always say, I do not even play in the NBA). It is a huge ask to be a great dad. I will start this chapter by saying that all of my kids have great moms!

Yes, divorce is tough and all that comes with it (visitation and money), but it will work out. For years, so many of my successful friends would call me after their separations and ask for advice on how to fix their current mess. (They considered me the expert after having gone through the process multiple times.) Most of these guys are what we in the business world call "Fixers"; they want the divorce to be settled in a day, just like they fix their business. Well, I have some unwelcome news. This is a process, and the divorce lawyers do not make it easier. It is their job to prolong the process for as long as possible to get paid the most. Most of these lawyers are well intended, but it is a business for them too. All of these divorce lawyers know each other, trading one nasty letter after another to satisfy their respective clients while inching the ball forward ever so slowly.

The bottom line is that divorce is a process that takes time. While that time passes, stay positive and constructive. Throw your energy

Words We Love to Hear

into enjoying your kids and your kids enjoying you. Soon you will discover that the basketball game or soccer game you never had time for before, suddenly you can now find the time. Enjoy watching your kids become adults.

I do not know what life would be like raising kids in a forty-year marriage. I only can tell from having a ringside seat watching some of my friends. I believe that for me personally I was a much better divorced dad than a married dad. As a divorced dad, I want to stay connected to my kids and be there for them all the time, both emotionally and financially. I must tell you it was a blast. Today with iPhones and Facetime, the connections are instantaneous and easy.

People say "He is a great dad." How hard is that? It is so much fun to watch a person start as an infant and blossom into an adult. Yes, there are problems along the way, but if you stay the course then you get to look back on all those times in your kid's life and laugh about their crazy escapades, how you punished them and their acceptance and reactions to their consequences. Now at my age, most of my friends have kids, and their kids are seeing all the joy, trials, and tribulations of being a parent. They finally understand the meaning of the words "mom" and "dad" and all the joy, laughter, and responsibilities that go with it.

As I am writing this chapter, I am in Philadelphia for my son's high school musical production of *The Addams Family*, where he has a starring role. I flew up from my home in Florida yesterday for the play. How much friggin' fun is that? That does not qualify as being a great dad; it qualifies as fun, at seeing this young man try so hard and perform so beautifully in his role. Sitting down as the lights dim and hearing the band kick off with *The Addams Family* theme song *(dom dom dom, dada dada...)* gets you in such a great mood. Then your child comes out and blows you out of your chair. How cool is that? You observe the energy he puts into his performance, the smile on his face, and the camaraderie with his fellow actors and actresses in the play. What an experience and a life lesson about teamwork, absolute personal satisfactions, following directions, and the resolve of watching the theatergoers thoroughly enjoy the cast's performance.

My twenty-one-year-old son went to the show with me and brought his girlfriend, which made it even more rewarding, as I observed the play through his eyes, smiling as he enjoyed watching his younger brother perform. My older son had been in his high school jazz band; he understood the nuisances of what goes into a performance like *The Addams Family* and the sophistication of a high school production. I will never forget the final jazz concert during his senior year. His music teacher came out on stage to introduce the thirty-piece jazz band and held up a blank sheet of paper. "This is what the band started with eight months ago," he said. "Tonight, you will see what these kids did with this blank sheet of paper." At that moment, the band started playing the great Frank Sinatra song "My Way." It almost makes you cry to think that this is your kid and his accomplishment of being on a "team" called a jazz band.

The next night, my older son and I went to the Philadelphia basketball game with the new star player, James Harden, whose sheer energy completely turned the franchise around. Harden, a seasoned thirty-two-year-old veteran making $46 million dollars per year, was traded to the team four games ago. What an incredible game! The arena (called the Wells Fargo Center) was packed to the rafters and the crowd was going insane. The energy was explosive! The 76ers were down by nineteen and came back to win the game in the last five minutes. There was pandemonium.

The highlight in the game came when a 76er player went to dunk the ball and was fouled and knocked on the ground under the basket. James Harden, who was thirty feet away past mid court, saw his teammate laying there after the hard foul. Harden runs as fast as he can to his teammate on the ground and extends his hand to pull the young man up off the floor. Incredible! James Harden is an old pro making $46 million balloons a year; he could just hang out at mid court for the next play. But he doesn't, because he is a leader. His actions showed his team he was not going to let up and lose. He is a winner, and his teammates are winners. This simple action of running full speed from half court and reaching out his hand to help his teammate changed the entire momentum of the game. His teammates believed they were truly one and were going to win. Guess what? They won five minutes after that happened. Everyone got behind the old veteran knowing that James Harden could have waited for the next play and still collected his $46 million dollar salary. Instead, his actions said, "I am special, my team is special, and I am going to be an example and hopefully everyone will understand that I am willing to do the challenging work and be a team player to win this game." That is leadership! That is motivation in the silent sense of the word.

CHAPTER 3

Do the Opposite Day

ᴏf the best TV shows in my lifetime were *Seinfeld* and *Curb Your ₣nthusiasm*. The entire concept of both of these shows was how life is ᵣeal and the real problems in life. There are so many *Seinfeld* episodes, but one of the greatest of all times was called "The Opposite." In the show, there is this character named George. For all intents and purposes George is a loser. He is thirty-six years old, overweight, bald, and generally unemployed through a good part of the show. In some episodes, he lives with his parents because being unemployed does not generate much income and he needs a roof over his head.

In this episode, George meets his friends at their usual meeting spot, a dumpy dinner in the neighborhood. Opining to his friends about how lousy his life is, his friend Jerry advises George that, since everything is going so bad for him, why not try to do the opposite of everything he does in his routine. The server comes over and Georges orders an egg salad sandwich instead of his usual chicken salad sandwich. He feels great making this change.

Next, Jerry convinces him to talk to a gorgeous girl who is eating at the counter. George laughs and says he'd have no chance but then goes up to her and introduces himself with brutal honesty. The girl finds this refreshing and agrees to a date.

Do the Opposite Day

So, what do we learn from George? Easy! When you are in a rut and things just are not going the way you envision them, change things up—change your approach, change your mindset, and believe that new things are about to happen. George was forever taking... hiding his true self. When George finally decides to "come clean," guess what? Things flipped 100% around. After George dates this girl, he goes on a job interview for an office job with the Yankees, same exact thing happens. Obviously, no one can go around life ... this all the time, but there is a balance that you can achieve. When you are in a rut, it is time to change things up and take another approach, just as a football coach adjusts his game at halftime. If the game plan is not working and you are losing at football, or at life, you need to adjust make things go better.

The show *Curb your Enthusiasm* has this character, Larry David, who perceives life as about being completely honest and transparent. Basically, saying things that everyone is thinking but no one has the guts to say aloud. Larry is a social assassin who calls out the silliness in society that most people are too scared to. In life, we tend to sugarcoat everything; only in our most intimate relationships do we tell the truth or say exactly what we are feeling. Life would be a little better if we approached things in a more honest and forthright manner.

There are so many examples of these frustrations every day of your life. Let's say that you are in a rush: You are in line at the supermarket in the ten-item or less line and the person in front of you has fifteen items. Would not you love to say, "Excuse me, you have too many items." To exacerbate this, the person then engages in a five-minute conversation with the cashier about nothing. You want to scream your head off! Larry David would do exactly what you are thinking of doing, but not doing. Confront the inconsiderate bastards and say, "You know this is a ten-item line for a reason. It's to move quickly, and you are doing anything but that!"

No one looks in the rear-view mirror of life; everyone just looks in front of themselves. We all have been in the situation where we are driving a car and the person in front of us has no idea anyone is behind them. They switch lanes, slow down to look for a street, stop in the middle of the block, swerve all over the road. This is how life is; no one looking behind to see the history or understand what is happening. Most people only have a fifty-percent view of life, looking forward and missing the details and ramifications of the past.

Don't you love this one? You go to a dinner party, and there is always some putz who does not shut up, usually a know-it-all. This person either talks about themselves all night or monopolizes the conversation. Certainly, if you are in a group and one of the people is famous or a great scholar or business mind, you would understand them controlling the conversation. More times than not it is a know-it-all idiot who will not shut up and drowns everyone out all evening. These people are usually narcissistic morons who are in love hearing themselves talk and, in most instances, convincing themselves that what they say is correct. A great social assassin like Larry David would tell that person exactly what you are thinking. "Shut up and let other people talk! No one wants to hear you all night!"

CHAPTER 4

Perception: One of the Keys to Success

Mental strength. How you perceive a situation in every person is similar and different. No matter who you are in all levels of society—rich or poor—one of the most humiliating experiences is standing at a host station on a Saturday night trying to get a table in a busy restaurant. You could be the CEO of a business, but unless you know someone at this restaurant or have a reservation, or are simply famous, you are going to be waiting and waiting for a crappy table.

I have this friend. For the purpose of this book, let us call him Dan. Over twenty years ago, I moved from the Jersey shore to the Hamptons for the summer. The Hamptons is commonly referred to as "Land of the Giants" by many Wall Street folks. Anyway, my friend Dan lived there for over twenty years and was very familiar with the nuances of the various towns and restaurants.

I said, "Dan, how am I ever going to get into these restaurants with all these giants out here?"

Do you know what his response was? "How are they going to keep you out!"

That is mental toughness, Ronald Reagan style. In Dan's mind, there was no chance that when he approached the host stand and talked to the manager, that they were not going to give him a table. Is it the confident manner in which he talks to the host? Is it the $20 bill he hands the manager? Is it his appearance? I would say it is all three and more. Bottom line, I have never seen him wait or be turned away. His attitude is such that he lets the manager know that being turned down is a nonstarter and that the manager is going to wear out faster than Dan.

I remember one weekend I was getting into a philosophical discussion with Dan over his approach to life. His response was that his work is extremely hard and challenging, and he approaches his "off time" with whatever it takes to enjoy that time stress-free. For example, Dan tips 50%! Sounds insane, right? Here is his explanation.

Dan goes to the same ten spots or stays at the same hotels in New York, Florida, or California, wherever he vacations. He wants the people who work there to treat him with respect, which he gives back in kind in two ways: being appreciative and friendly and, of course, his theory of excess tipping.

Let us say that a standard tip is 20%. Dan tips 50%, or 30% more than the standard. Assume he goes out 100 times a year, which sounds like a lot. Each time the average cost, between lunch and dinner, is $125 for two people ($200 for dinner, $50 for lunch). Multiply this by 100 times per year (365 days or one-third of your days) and you will spend $12,500 total. Dan explains that if you then use the multiple of an extra 30% in tips over the normal standard tip amount, you will expend an extra $3,750 per year being an excess tipper. Now every place you go, they fall all over you because you are the best tipper coming into their restaurant. To put this in perceptive, you could spend $1,000 or more for a suit, $10,000 or more per year leasing a car, $6,000 a year for cable or a cell phone, $15,000 or more for a vacation. The simple act of being the biggest tipper in a restaurant will enhance your life, change your experiences, and bring you a stress-free environment to enjoy your down time—all for a measly $3,750 per year.

Now, let us assume that you have a big lifestyle; your numbers are double or triple the above example. (It is all relative because your income and lifestyle expense are also double or triple.) For example, if you stay in a five-star hotel or take a few private flights per year, this excess tipping model is a fraction of your life but will bring you the most amount of joy—over many lunches and dinners, or even while parking your car. Never waiting for a table in a restaurant or a car in a valet line is precious. I have a billionaire friend who has a favorite expression: "I can make money. I cannot make time." So true. When you are not working, you want to enjoy and relax with zero stress.

The above is one of the great secrets of life that I personally have employed since my friend Dan shared it with me. What a difference it makes in all aspects of life. Plus, there's that extra special component of making someone who works their butt off in the service industry, incredibly happy and satisfied with your generosity. This model is very gratifying to both you and the people in the service industry.

CHAPTER 5
The Skill of Observation

Observation is one of the most underutilized tools in the toolshed. How many times have you been sitting at an airport, a ballgame, or even a shopping mall, and you sit there and people-watch? Everyone does it. You decide what and who people are based upon your observation. The truth of the matter is that so many things can be learned from an observation.

Today, I was in the parking lot of the gym I go to every morning. I parked next to a car that I see in the lot every morning at 5:30. There is only about six or eight cars there in the morning, and I'm curious who owns this car. Does the car belong to one of the crazy guys who go in at 5:30, or does it belong to one of the girls who is there at 5:30? In any case, it is in the same spot every day, in the front row. Here is where observation comes into play. I parked next to this car every morning. The car is five years old. Without being a creep, I can see inside the car window because. As I exit or get into my car, I am one foot away from the car window. There is a realtor sticker on the back of the car from one of the larger real estate offices in town, so I now assume that this car is owned by a realtor. There is a ton of open house flyers in the car, another indication that the car owner is a realtor. I decide not to stare in the window to see whose picture is on the realtor open house flyer. I instead try and just figure it out by other tactics. Having just started at the gym a few months earlier, I had a run

The Skill of Observation

in with a women, and I'm wondering if it's her car. This car is next to me every day when there are over one hundred empty spots in the lot this early in the morning.

I have never been in a gym in my life, and it being a new experience I did not know gym protocol. I start out on the treadmills that overlook the weightlifting equipment and face forward I watch everyone lifting weights. There is this one woman with a Jennifer Lopez or Kim Kardashian type rear end that I watch workout every morning just because the equipment is right in front of me

One day after the treadmill, I go over to the weights, and the weights are in between her and the mirror she is staring into as she lifts weights. Not knowing what to do, I jump in front of her, excuse myself, and grab my weight. At that this women blurts out, "You are a dirty old man. I catch you staring at my ass everyday. I'm reporting you to management." I can't believe it. I have tried to stay out of trouble my entire life and found nothing but trouble by what I believe is a misunderstanding. Here, I'm new in the gym, trying to get in shape for the first time in my life, and within weeks I'm getting reported to management. I wonder is this the girl who parks next to me every day.Just from parking next to this car, I can see through the window that the inside of the car is a mess with stuff everywhere. I guess I can assume that this person is not so neat. Then, standing outside of the car, I can see makeup everywhere on the front seat. I guess I can then assume that this car is owned by a woman who puts her makeup on in the car, maybe because she is running late. (I personally hate when people are late). Based upon these observation, I limit the women down in the gym to a few, and I now have a good idea who it could be because the equipment is very close together, and you cannot help but hear people's conversation. There is one woman who is always talking about houses that she either is listing or showing, so I know she is a realtor.

This woman is in the gym working out hard every morning. Again, I can assume she is determined and wants to maintain her body in the best possible shape. She works out every day with whoever is in the gym and talks to everyone, I guess to promote her real estate business and brand, trying to interact with as many people as possible hoping to find new clients.

Now, let us just recap this one experience. From observation, I can now assume the following things about this woman: She is not organized, nor is she neat. She is a businesswoman and a realtor. She is obviously always late by the thought of putting her makeup on while driving to the gym. She is extremely concerned about her appearance and works hard at her age to maintain her figure and stay in shape. She loves to talk and network and is interested in networking and advancing her career. I see no rings on her fingers or any conversation about a boyfriend or husband, but nothing can be determined from that, as a lot of women at the gym do not wear wedding or engagement rings, and many do because the want men to stay away. In this case, it is unclear, as this women is an aggressive realtor and wants business so she does want a reason for people to reject her immediately. I do see her make a group of friends, and then for some strange reason there is a conflict, so she moves on to another group of people. Most people in the gym are not there to make friends. They go in, they are nice, they work out, and they leave. This woman has a different agenda, so I'm thinking she is the one who turned me into management. I never found out and did not get in trouble, so who cares.

Wow, that is amazing how much I learned about this woman by just observing.

The Skill of Observation

There are many things we can learn about people just by observing them from a distance. Going out to dinner with another couple, it is easy to figure out if they like each other and get along. I have a friend that is not openly nice to his wife in front of other people. They have been married for over thirty years, and obviously the love has worn off, but he does not have to be abusive. By this observation, I can tell that this guy is a bully and is not really a good guy. If you do not like your wife, then leave. Do not abuse her. This guy is also overweight. I assume he is not happy with himself or his life and that he eats and drinks to medicate himself. For some reason, he is not interested in working out or going on a diet and assumes diminishing others will make him feel better. This is purely speculation, but I also assume that, being a large guy, he is a bully in every part of his life.

There are many examples of how observing people or places can help you define who they are without even knowing them or, even if you do know them, how observing them will help you know them better. It is important to look up, down, and all around to try and understand the circumstances. Let us say that you get off a train in a strange city and observe all around you plight and poverty. This observation will lead you to believe that you remove any jewelry and be very aware of your surroundings for your safety. You must be constantly diligent of your surroundings and the people around you in this extremely dangerous world.

Out of all the chapters in this book, if you take one thing away and use it daily it will be the art of observation. People use the art of observation, but do not even realize it. Observation of people, places, and things will help you survive and thrive. Use this tool to your best advantage. As soon as you realize that observation is an unbelievably valuable tool, you will pay attention more and use it to improve your life.

CHAPTER 6

Stature Is the "IT" Factor

You can tell when someone has the "It" factor! It is simply their stature or the way they carry themselves when they walk into a room or a gym or anywhere for that matter. There is an old expression: "Lead, follow, or get out of the way." That is so true in life.

Every morning at 5 a.m., I go to a big gym near my house. After making a quick stop at Starbucks for some caffeine, I pull my car into the gym parking lot at 5:30 a.m. I am astonished at how many cars are already in the lot!

I start my work out every morning on the third floor overlooking the gym. From my treadmill, I can see everyone walking up the steps to the main floor. It is the same people, the same trainers, every morning with the exception of a few new faces. You can tell which trainers are wildly successful. They have the "It" factor that attracts people to them. Whatever it is—their build, their sense of fashion, their hair—most people can instantly tell who is cool and who is not. The guy I train with in the gym is short and skinny; he has giant arms, a shaved head, and three-day old beard all the time (how does it look three-days old every day?) and just a kick-ass attitude from the jump! Guess what? After I got to know this guy, I soon discovered his history: He was a former UFC fighter. I could tell when I met him by his stature—the way he looked, the way he talked, the way he walked—that he commanded a presence. First thing I said to this guy was, "I want arms like you have. How did you get them?" His response, "Would you go to a dentist with bad teeth? This is what I do for a living. Would you want me to train you to get big arms if I had skinny little arms?" So true.

There is another group, three guys and one girl, that trains together every morning. The way they move from equipment to equipment, the way they walk around the gym, there is an order as to who goes first, second, etc. It is stature. I do not know how they rank, but in the gym, there is a leader and followers on what they are going to do in the way of the workout for the day. The leader has a big voice and big muscles, and they are mentally tough at this workout game. The followers want to be just like him, at least in this gym world. The guy carries stature.

Why do I go to a gym, everyone asks? "You live in a mansion," they say, "and have a workout room nicer than any gym." The answer is motivation, camaraderie, and a sense of being part of a team.

Every morning when I climb out of bed at 5 a.m., I say to myself (especially after a night of three tequila martinis) "I cannot do this today." The truth of the matter is that it is hard to get to the gym; it is even harder to leave. I move slowly around my bedroom. I wash my face and put my gym stuff on saying, "Just get in the car." I swig some pomegranate juice, grab a banana, and get in my car. I have a bunch of nice cars, and it is always fun driving one first thing in the morning to "set the tone and attitude for the day." I get the Warren Buffett attitude—drive a used old car—it works for him, not me. I need to get motivated and feel good first thing in the morning. Getting in a fresh, nice-smelling, clean and fancy car starts my day off with a great attitude.

I get to the 7-Eleven at 5:15 a.m. and buy my two papers. It is the same overnight guy there with a great attitude, dreadlocks and all. My papers cost $4.56. I hand him a $10 bill every morning and tell him to keep the change. There is always a bellowing, "Thank you, brother. Have an enjoyable day!" Then it's off to Starbucks and the gym. At the gym there are muscle men, skinny women, fat women, fat men, and everyone in between. It is incredible motivation to see the same faces at 5:30 a.m., knowing that others are making the same sacrifices as you to stay healthy.

There is a woman who must weigh 225 pounds or more, but every morning she is there working out and sweating, trying her best to get healthy. Another woman works out next to me on the treadmill, running so fast for almost one hour that it motivates me to move faster on my treadmill. There is a guy with one leg who lifts weights, working out his upper body. Another guy, a former Marine with a million tattoos is huge and overweight, but I watch this tough Marine do chin-ups every morning. Do you know how hard it is to do a chin-up? I cannot imagine the strength this Marine has to lift his body and do a chin-up. This is why I go to the gym. It is incredibly motivating to be in this environment and see all these people struggle (certainly more than I do) to get through their daily regimen. Afterward, these folks walk out the front door satisfied that they made it through another workout. One day at a time, they say to themselves.

Growing up, I was required to take a mandatory sport in the tenth grade. One sport was wrestling. I took it only because the wrestling coach also owned the overnight camp where all the local kids went in the summer. His name was Uncle Steve, and he might have been one of the baddest guys I ever met in my life. Uncle Steve stood five feet, one inch tall, but in my eyes, he was a monster. The way he walked

Stature Is the "IT" Factor

into a room, the way he talked to a crowd, the way he carried himself, he had stature. I remember first engaging Uncle Steve in the wrestling room. I thought I was a wise guy and I said to him, "You are a little short guy. What is that you know to have this? Is it attitude, karate, jujitsu, or what?" Uncle Steve looked at me straight in the eye and said in an aggressive tone, "I know crazy." I knew this guy meant it. If you told me he bit off someone's nose, I would understand. From that moment, I knew that Uncle Steve was the real deal—he was legitimate tough and crazy all, five feet, one inch of him.

For the ten years or so that we all went to summer camp, Uncle Steve ran it with an iron grip! It was immensely fun, but there was a line. You could go up to the line, you could dance on the line, but God save you if you crossed Uncle Steve's line. The one thing you knew for sure was you were going to have fun and be safe. Every day, Uncle Steve drove a golf cart around the camp, visiting each of the activities. When he pulled up to your baseball game or soccer game, something about just looking at this five-feet, one-inch guy made you feel confident, lucky, and most importantly, safe.

Uncle Steve had a half-brother, Jimmy. His brother was not involved in the camp but I guess on some level had some ownership. He would come up to the camp a couple times during the summer, but he was not active enough to know anything about this guy other than the fact that he was big... Six foot three big or at least a foot taller than Uncle Steve. Jimmy besides being tall was a big-frame guy who I assumed played sports his entire life.

Do you know how certain things stick out in your life that you always remember? Well, at the end of my years at summer camp, Uncle Steve got pancreatic cancer. As he drove around camp in his golf cart that last year, you could see the cancer eating alive the toughest guy I ever met. He was shrinking away daily before our eyes. Uncle Steve never let you know he was sick or in excruciating pain with a terminal disease. He was a tough guy through and through. He made you feel safe while he was alive, and God forbid the day when he was gone. His confident personality was contagious, especially when he was sick. When you thought you could not do another round of weights or last another quarter at basketball in the heat, all you had to do was think of Uncle Steve climbing out of his golf cart, his body riddled with cancer as he walked thirty yards just to say hello and offer a few words of encouragement for the last quarter of the game. He was a life lesson in grit, determination, and motivation.

When camp ended a month later, Uncle Steve died of pancreatic cancer. Everyone went to the funeral. We all knew there was no way this pancreatic cancer was going to kill Uncle Steve before the end of summer camp. The cancer was afraid of him, at least for a few more weeks till he said his goodbyes for the summer. Jimmy, Uncle Steve's brother, gave the eulogy. I will never forget it, even fifty years later. Jimmy stood at the podium and told us that he was six feet, three inches and 263 pounds.

Then he looked at the open casket of his brother and said, "I never felt so safe walking down a street late at night in center city Philadelphia than with my brother, all five feet, one inch of him." He continued, "If there was trouble on the street, I was in the safest place in town—standing next to my brother."

Everyone in the audience knew precisely what Jimmy was saying. Uncle Steve was mentally tough and confident; he had such stature that being in his presence gave you a complete sense of safety and reassurance. If we can get a little piece of that mojo, then life will be so much more rewarding in every way. I think about Uncle Steve often and try and emulate his infectious confidence.

That brings me back to the title of this book, "Survival Guide for Business and Life: Head Down—Left Foot, Right foot." That was Uncle Steve all through his life and especially at the end. He kept his head held high and took one step at a time, punching and walking to the end of life. As I underwent problems in life and in business, Uncle Steve popped into my mind to give me the energy and inspiration to slug through the mess and get to the other side. It has always worked well.

CHAPTER 7
Gone in Sixty Seconds

The canvas of life is littered with the greats who destroyed their lives in sixty seconds. How is that possible? To be one of the greatest of all time and completely blow it in a matter of minutes. The list is a long one: Charlie Sheen, Phil Mickelson, Mike Tyson, Mel Gibson, Will Smith, Lindsay Lohan, Richard Nixon, and on and on. All of these people have one thing in common; they were great and on top of the world, and then they lost control and did something stupid and the world took them down. Only a few greats survived their indiscretions. The one that immediately comes to mind is Tiger Woods. This man had to battle back from beyond zero, but he had humility and was willing to immediate recognize his indiscretion and get back on the horse. The world loved him; it told him to go stand in the corner for a while and then it brought him back. The only reason Tiger was allowed to come back from his indiscretion was that he realized his mistakes immediately and took full responsibility for them. He did not hide or try and blame others; he said, "I screwed up. This is all on me."

As I write this chapter, there are mistakes happening with two of the greatest of all time.

The first is Phil Mickelson, one of the greatest golfers of all time with forty-five wins on the tour and six major championships. That is a monumental level of accomplishments for a career spanning thirty years. To quickly summarize, Phil made a very inappropriate comment about the PGA tour in an interview. Then, he made things worse by stating that he might leave the PGA and join the Saudi middle east tour. Saudi Arabia is well known for their human rights abuses. With this comment and interview alone, the American PGA Tour suspended Phil Mickelson and all of his sponsors yanked their support and association with him. What was he thinking? He had worked his ass off for thirty years, became the darling of the golf world, was making hundreds of millions of dollars in golf and endorsement earnings, and these egregious comments from one interview destroyed his life! It's hard to imagine a smart guy like that having a brain fart so horrific.

Now we turn to Will Smith. What an idiot. In 2022, Smith attended the Oscars, hopefully to accept his first academy award for the movie King Richard. Will and his wife are sitting in the first few rows in front of the Oscar stage. (Nominees must be seated upfront so that if they win, they do not have to wander through all the tables to get to the stage.) The Oscars are broadcast around the world and the time it takes to give and accept the awards is precious.

Many of the presenters at these awards shows are comedians. In this case, the presenter was Chris Rock, who made an off-color joke about Will Smith's wife, Jada. Instead of taking the joke as "it goes with the territory," Will stood up, walked onto the stage, and slapped Chris Rock in front of a worldwide audience of millions of people. To add insult to injury, he then used profanity directed at Chris Rock. This is assault and battery! In a civil society, you cannot do this. Can you imagine being at a basketball game, sitting on the floor and screaming at the players, and the coach says to you "shut up" so you go and slap the coach? Not only would you be thrown out of the arena on your ass, you would be locked up.

The fallout from this incident is just happening now. Will Smith will be shunned by Hollywood and be poison for doing something so stupid. I guess for society's sake this was a Black-on-Black assault. Can you imagine if either one of these giant stars were white? The craziness in our society would have been out of control and endless blaming each side for causing this stupidity.

I could continue this chapter with all of the greats who have screwed up their entire careers in a sixty-second moment of bad judgment. In life, you never ever can let your guard down when you are in the public eye. At home, you can walk around naked and scream your lungs out, but when you are in a public setting—it could be the Oscars or a school board meeting—you always must have total control of your anger and rage. Think about these two guys who worked their entire lives to be the biggest and the greatest in their field and in sixty seconds threw it all away. As my brother-in-law always said to the kids, "Sit on your hands for the night and go home and go to bed. Tomorrow, you will figure it out." Rage is dangerous and all of the motivation and reading of books like this one will not help if you lose control of your rage and throw your life away in sixty seconds.

CHAPTER 8
Thank You for Your Service

The other day, I drove from my home in Palm Beach, Florida to Captiva Island on the western coast. It is about a three-hour ride across the state on one road called Alligator Alley. There is nothing to see for three hours but the swamps that alligators live in.

I am driving behind a Mustang going fifteen miles per hour in a twenty-five-mile zone, with about two miles to go. This went on for about one mile. After the mustang pulled off, I floored my truck and in twenty seconds I was pulled over by a police officer. Can you believe this? I am one mile from the resort having driven three hours to get there, and I get pulled over! There must be a technique where the police officer is able to shine a huge light directly into your sideview mirror that blinds you until the officer is right at the driver's side mirror.

The officer approached my truck looking for a fight. He was aggressive and big; the vest, the gun, and all the stuff he wears is very intimidating. I had my license out, and when he was at my window, I said, "Officer, thank you for your service. I'm sorry for what you guys are going through." At that, it was like someone let the air out of a balloon.

The officer seemed a little calmer. In a loud voice, he said, "You know the speed limit is twenty-five-miles-per-hour here, and you are doing forty."

I responded, "Officer, I am not looking to argue. I appreciate your service. If you say I was going forty, then I was."

The officer was flabbergasted at my response. He took my driver's license and said, "Let me check you out. I will be right back." The officer comes back about two minutes later and says, "I figured a guy driving a Lamborghini SUV at 9 p.m. at night would be an asshole, but you had nothing but respect and acceptance of your speed, so tonight is your lucky night. Drive your last mile slowly and have a pleasant vacation."

What did I learn? A lot! I could have given him a story about the Mustang or said something stupid like "Do you know who I am?" or "What is your badge number?" He would have pulled me out of the car or given me a speeding ticket at the minimum. Instead, I put my ego aside, ate some humble pie, and gave the officer the respect he deserves. He felt good, and I felt better.

This is such an important lesson in life. In most situations, there is someone who has control over you. It could be a banker or a police officer, or it could be a judge or a spouse, or even the host in a restaurant where you desperately want a table. Respecting that individual will go a long way. The goal is to win and maintain your stature as a successful person but do it in a respectful way so that it does not come across as arrogant. By virtue of the fact that I was in a rare and expensive car, I had the stature of a successful person to this officer. In this case, the car worked against me. When I showed the officer respect and thanked him for his service, the car worked to my advantage. This officer had a preconceived notion I was going to be some rich asshole, but when he realized I was just a regular person who was speeding and was remorseful of my mistake, the officer was disarmed and had to let me go. I believe that in life, this lesson can be applied to almost any tricky situation. If you can check your ego at the door, you can win with dignity. The police officer already knew that I was rich, so there was no point shoving it in his face. As it turns out, after he let me go, we had a five-minute conversation about the war in Ukraine, as Officer Lust was a former Marine (super interesting guy). I learned a great lesson about how easy it is to get what you want and need by being nice. This was not brown-nosing; it was done with stature and respect. It was immediately clear to me that if I disrespected this officer, it would have been an extremely long and uncomfortable evening.

Your ego can be your best friend, and at times it can be your worst friend. Most people are afraid to eat "humble pie" because of their ego. What everyone fails to understand is if you win by checking your ego, then it is a victory no matter how your ego feels going through the process.

What I understood, and what the officer did not understand, was that when I was getting pulled over, I knew I had the advantage, not the officer. Yes, he had the badge and the law on his side, but I had stature and humility on my side. The officer had no argument because I did nothing but respect him and his position and I excepted responsibility for my actions. This officer knew that, if he wrote me a ticket, I was going to hire some big shot lawyer to get me out of it. The officer did a fast equation. I was respectful and appreciative. Writing a ticket would have done nothing. The officer would have had to come to court and deal with some Perry Mason-type lawyer getting in his face with the case thrown out or the penalty reduced. The officer did the math and figured it out.

Two people won that day, and that is how it should be. The officer won because some rich big shot totally respected him, appreciated his work, and thanked him sincerely for his service in a dangerous world. I won because I got to meet a real hero and a nice human being and to create a new memory and real-life experience to add to my book.

At the beginning of my career, I used to go to township meetings to get the land I was going to build on through the approval process. My attorney never wanted me to go to the nighttime meetings because he always wanted to tell the board of commissioners that he had to check with Mr. Cutler in the morning for a response. I always wanted to go because I did not understand that my lawyer's approach was the best approach. After a year or two went by and I had been to countless meetings I understood it was a disadvantage for me to be in attendance.

When going to the meetings, I always drove up in a regular car like a Buick. It is so funny in life that people always notice the car you drive up in and have a preconceived notion of who you are. If you drive a fancy car to a strip club, chances are that you will get in the VIP section. The same goes for a fancy restaurant. If you pull up to the valet in a fancy car, the chances are that the host will know they will get a big tip. Crazy how the system works. Cars speak a secret language.

As I sat there and listened to the board of commissioners abuse my attorney, I watched this brilliant lawyer take every punch in a low-key way. The first couple of times I went, I wondered why my seasoned lawyer would take such a pounding by the board of commissioners, who got a simple pleasure out of being bullies. My lawyer made great points, all of it made common sense, but he never got emotional or lost his cool. (If it were me in my earlier days, I would go up there and probably punch one of the arrogant commissioners in the face.)

After a couple of meetings with this abuse and my lawyer taking these punches in the face, I watched the vote. We won the zoning vote: 6 to 0. I looked at my lawyer and saw a small smirk on his face.

As we walked into the parking lot, we started laughing. Yes, they did humiliate and embarrass us in public, and it was not fun, but how hard did it hurt? We would now make millions of dollars building exactly what we wanted to on this piece of ground at the expense of a few nasty humiliating comments. The goal was to win, to do well and succeed, to get across the finish line in one piece with a victory in hand—and this was a big victory. It does not always have to go like that, but in most cases it does. This is life for most people. Some days or weeks, it can feel like walking in mud; it's difficult to lift your legs. In the end, you always get where you are going. It just may take more time and effort.

CHAPTER 9

Never Judge a Book by Its Cover

There is an adage that never seems to get old, but for some reason or another you always fall for it. Several years ago, I was at a Starbucks getting coffee, just vegging out on the sofas on a rainy Saturday morning in Florida. For years, I have tried and succeeded in not allowing anyone to take a picture of me for fear it would end up on the internet; then every person who was trying to sell me something would know what I looked like. One thing I value in life is privacy, peace, and quiet, because I really have a tough time saying no and I always get myself into uncomfortable situations. Today was no different. I value my days off, the quiet regrouping and getting ready for another Monday when the world comes at you full force.

So many times, I'll be sitting at Starbucks, enjoying my delicious Saturday hot coffee, staring at my copy of the New York Post, when I see out of the corner of my eye some guy starting to approach me. I say to myself, "Jesus Christ," as he is now standing over me.

The man dressed in homeless attire asks me, "Are you David so and so? I am originally from Philadelphia, and my brother's cousin's second wife's son [or something like] introduced me to you that years ago." Of course, this guy who again looks homeless, says, "Do you mind if I sit down?"

He proceeds to sit down without me even answer, and he goes on to tell me his name, which means nothing to me, and starts to tell me how he, his wife, and two young children are living in a townhouse while they build this house up the street. I'm listening half-heartedly as he continues to tell me all the problems he is having with the construction of this new home and is lost as to what to do.

The next thing this guy says is, "How about we get a free refill and you look at my house and tell me what you think I should do? It is only a mile down the road." Ugh!

Figuring that it is some type of 2,000-square foot development home, and it is a rainy day with no golf, I say to myself, 'What the f–. Sure, let's go look at it. I have fifteen minutes."

I walk out of the Starbucks with... Let's call him Joe. He says, "Follow me," gets into a ten-year-old Range Rover, and off we go. About a mile down the road, Joe pulls up to a chain link fence and gets out to take off the padlock. As I drive in, I am floored by the sight of a truly magnificent, 25,000-foot mansion set on a gorgeous intercoastal lot on one of the nicest streets in Boca Raton. This property, when finished, had to be a thirty-million-dollar plus home. As I walk through this eighty-percent completed property, I kicked myself for being such a loser that I didn't give this guy Joe his due at Starbucks just because of his clothes and his beard. Instead of taking this man at face value, and thinking it could be anyone, including Warren Buffett's son, I had a preconceived impression that this guy could barely afford the Starbucks coffee, let alone be building a thirty-million-dollar home. As we wandered through this incredible property with its incredible view, out of curiosity I started asking this guy, "Who are you?"

Well, he proceeds to tell me that he invented the air and vacuum concession at all the gas stations around the East Coast of the U.S. He eventually sold that off and became one of the angel investors in PayPal and some other venture capital business, besides becoming a huge real estate investor. Furthermore, to make me feel like a bigger idiot, he shows me a picture of his gorgeous wife, who is a famous surgeon in Miami! To this day, the two of us remain friends. His house, now completed, is truly one of the more gorgeous homes in South Florida. Every day when I come home from the gym, I pass his house with its gorgeous, manicured landscaping, and cannot help but think of our first meeting and remember, "Never judge a book by its cover!"

* * *

I remember much earlier in my life that my dad had a friend, Bob. Both my dad and Bob were retired, and they played golf every day. Bob was a handsome guy, but he was at least one hundred pounds overweight. He was poorly dressed due to the fact that it was difficult to find proper golf attire that fit him.

Bob was always wearing baggy pants and a huge shirt that hung out of his pants. When I played golf with them, we always met Bob at the first tee, and other than pleasantries I really did not know anything about him except that he was a retired insurance agent. His golf cart was a big mess, just like him, with dozens of old golf balls everywhere, crap hanging out of the cart, and with two golf bags overfilled with dirty old clubs.

That summer, my father had a surprise birthday party in Philadelphia for my mother. Bob and his wife were invited. Throughout my entire career, I started work early. Our company always had one secretary that came in early and another that stayed late. At 6:45 a.m., the early secretary comes back to my office and tells me that there is some guy (Bob, my dad's friend) out front in the lobby and that he has a box of donuts for me. I said, "Bring him back to my conference room," figuring that Bob is here for the party and had nothing better to do, so why not go bother Dave?Bob bounces back into the conference room wearing a nicer-than-usual outfit and I invite him to sit down. Obviously, he is in town for the surprise party tomorrow and is just killing time, figuring he would come over to my office and waste an hour of my Friday morning. I always enjoyed playing golf with Bob and his company, so to sit here and drink coffee and have a chocolate-filled donut, which I almost never eat, sounded like a fun way to start the day rather than fighting with contractors.

I engaged in a conversation with Bob that I never really had with him when it was just golf. Once again, boy was I wrong! Who was Bob before he retired? He was the largest Lloyds of London insurance agent in the U.S. If you were a jeweler, or anyone who had a high-value item and you needed insurance, you had to go to Lloyds of London, the finest insurance agency in the world for valuable items. And if you were in New York, you had to use Bob. For the next three hours, this man told me the most incredible stories of the rich and famous and the heists of their jewelry or artwork. It was so exciting—these almost James Bond-like episodes of how items were stolen, and sometimes recovered, and how Bob dealt with the claims. I will never forget those three hours.

The best story Bob told me was about when he was in New York. He was much thinner, always wore a gorgeous Brioni suit and tie, and had a driver. When he retired, he gained weight, got rid of the driver, and started wearing what he called "sloppy golf wear with stains from breakfast or lunch all over it from the finest dumps in all South Florida," as he put it.

Anyway, retired and now living in Florida full-time, Bob decides to treat himself to a Rolls Royce. After walking into the Rolls Royce dealership and asking several times to be helped, finally a young kid, green behind the ears, comes over and tells him that everyone is busy. He just started and does not know much, but will be happy to help. Bob assumes (correctly) that they took one look at him and figured he could not afford to fill the gas tank on a Rolls Royce, let alone buy one, so why waste any time? Guess what? Bob bought two Rolls Royces that day— a convertible and a four-door sedan. It was a quarter of the sales for this dealership for the month. When the young salesperson told the manager that Bob wanted to buy these two cars, the manager came over and tried to suck up to Bob. Guess what? Bob did not fall for it. He said he was happy to buy the cars from the kid and wanted to make sure the kid got the commissions for both cars, as it was his sale.

Joking, I said, "Bob, what is your secret sauce that made you so successful?" His answer was that he knew how people thought and therefore understood the game. I only tell this story now because Bob has passed away and it does not matter how he conducted his business.

Bob told me about a jeweler, a client in New York City, who had a $5-million-dollar robbery and immediately called Bob in a panic. Bob meets with the guy and says he will work on it, but he knows that the $5 million is the retail value, not this jeweler's cost. After about a month, the guy calls Bob in a panic and says he needs the money to buy inventory; he will take $3 million. Bob proceeds to tell him that he has received a $2-million-dollar settlement offer from the insurance company, but to hold off—he thinks he can get more. Meanwhile, Bob has secured a $4 million dollar settlement from the insurance company, but he does not let the jeweler know. The jeweler calls several weeks later and says he is desperate to settle. Bob now tells him that he has gotten the insurance company up to $3 million and will personally lend the jeweler $2 million dollars till the case is resolved, but hold off—Bob thinks he can get more money. The jeweler is relieved. A few weeks later, Bob calls the jeweler and says that he has a check in hand for $4 million dollars and that the case is settled. The jeweler thinks and knows that Bob got him more money than his cost and while negotiating that gave him personal funds for cash flow. This is how Bob became so gigantic. The jeweler told everyone he knew that Bob was the best insurance agent and that the cost to insure was not as important as the results of a claim. Bob would get new business from anyone the jeweler would speak to as a reference. This is how Bob conducted himself over for all the years in business, and this was his secret sauce. Bob got it. Since he retired and was no longer wearing the badge of a giant insurance magnet in a $5,000 suit, people treated him differently. He wore the change well.

The next evening at the party, I saw Bob dressed in a stunning suit with his silver hair blown dry to perfection. His gorgeous wife, who I had never met, had on the most amazing jewelry that I had ever seen. (Trust me, if she fell into a swimming pool, she would sink to the bottom she had so many diamonds on.) Jokingly, I said to Bob, "Wow, that's the most amazing jewelry I have ever seen." Bob smiled and told me that it was all stolen. When it was recovered, he was able to get a great price on it from his company! We both laughed hard! If three months earlier, on the first tee of a round of golf with my Pop and Bob, you told me this story was true. I would have never believed you.

Never judge a book by its cover. Both "Joe" and Bob ended up being wildly successful. Because of their appearance, I almost missed meeting two of the most interesting guys in my life. Now I assume that anyone I talk to could be super successful at anything they do—and that does not have to be money, it could be anything. A woman could be the best teacher or the best CEO; a man could be a renowned artist or a former world-class Olympian. You never know! So, judging a book by its cover could be a missed opportunity to learn something from someone who, in most cases, overcame their appearance to be or do something great. Always give everyone a fair chance to succeed or fail on their own. It is a huge mistake to make that judgment for them!

CHAPTER 10
The Importance of Shoes

Do you know what the number-one article of clothing is that a woman looks at on a man? Shoes!

Crazy, right? Who would ever think that? But it is true by unanimous vote. The general theme of appearance is so important in motivation and stature. What is appearance? Appearance does not mean wearing a suit and tie every day, but it does mean looking your best whatever your style is. If your style is a suit and tie, make sure your suit is clean, your shirt is crisp, and your shoes are shined. If you style is more casual, make sure your clothes are clean and neat. If your style is rugged, make sure it is a "classic" rugged through and through. Whenever you go out at night or go to work, it's important to put your best foot forward and make sure your appearance is up to par.

I do not know the psychology behind why the number-one article of clothing on a man is their shoes. I can only assume that it is the one constant that tells people you care about your appearance, and is possibly a clue to your economic status. Do not get me wrong—shoes do not tell someone if you are rich or poor, but they certainly speak to your efforts to look good and the fact that you have disposable money for that effort. For example, how many women place tremendous emphasis on their shoes? Women's shoes are fantastic, with all types of shapes and sizes of heels and different colors on the top and the

The Importance of Shoes

bottom of the shoe. Shoes make you feel taller and more statuesque. Why not give yourself the best chance, right off the get-go, by putting on a nice pair of shoes? It certainly gives one a great appearance and adds confidence first thing in the morning.

I wish people did not judge a book by its cover, but unfortunately most of us do. Someone can prepare for hours for a presentation, an interview, or even a date, and blow it in the first ten seconds by not looking sharp. You get one chance at a first impression—make it your best effort or you will spend the rest of the time in that presentation, interview, or date trying to convince people to come around to your idea that they like you or what you are saying. Why not start out strong with a great appearance rather than starting out behind the eight-ball looking sloppy and trying the rest of the time to overcome the bad karma at the start of your interaction.

Some people think it is cool to just show up. Wrong! Save that for being at home or hanging around out back. Look at some of the actors and actresses at the Hollywood award shows; they take a significant effort to look cool or spend a ton of time trying to appear distressed or sloppy. The same applies here. People try to make a great appearance to make a great impression. Whether that impression is to look cool and sharp or purposely sloppy in baggy clothes, a big effort is made either way. That effort always shows nicely.

Of primarily importance is personal hygiene. If you are going to walk around with a three-day beard on your face, do it right. If you are going to have some wild hairstyle, do it right. Make sure your teeth are clean and white. It is so easy to get a few Crest whitening strips at the drugstore and wear them for one hour a week. The difference in your look and smile is remarkable! Make sure you shower every single day. There is nothing worse than sitting next to someone who smells. If you have some extra money, there's nothing better than a little cologne or perfume. Not too much to knock someone over, but just enough that you smell clean and fresh. The conversation of personal hygiene is assumed and never talked about in motivation books. Bullshit. Personal hygiene is a huge conversation that should be discussed loudly and frequently as it tells a lot about a person. If someone cannot take care of themselves and what they look like, how are they going to be as a partner in both business and life? People spend a fortune on cars or pocketbooks. Take a little of that money and spend it on yourself to look sharp. It goes a long way.

CHAPTER 11
The Amazing Comeback

There are many great comeback stories that show how grit and determination are the clear definition of motivation for when you get kicked in the balls or are down and out.

The greatest of all time, Muhammad Ali, was suspended from boxing for years while he fought the draft to go to the Vietnam War. Muhammad made an amazing comeback to capture the world title.

George Forman retired and then at forty-eight-years old came back to capture the world title in heavyweight boxing as the oldest man to hold that title.

Boxer Mike Tyson had his world destroyed when he was convicted for rape and went to prison for three and half years. His chances of redeeming himself on the world stage were at zero. He came back to win the world title and somehow overcame all odds to now have a huge show business career.

Martha Stewart went to jail for insider trading and made a huge comeback in her career. The ultimate homemaker saw her reputation destroyed when she went to jail. She came out of prison, accepted responsibility of her actions, and redeemed herself with books and TV shows that branded the homemaking lifestyle everyone loves and wants.

The Amazing Comeback

Robert Downey Jr. ran afoul of the law and made an amazing comeback. As a heroin and cocaine addict, his life and career were over. Somehow, down-and-out Robert Downey Jr. faced all his demons and rebuilt his amazing career to be bigger and better than ever.

Ellen DeGeneres made a comeback after the world turned their back on her when she came out as a lesbian in her early sitcom years. With strength and determination in herself, she came back to have the highest-paid afternoon talk show on all of TV.

Michael Jordan quit basketball to play baseball after his father died. After that career fizzled out, he returned to basketball and became the greatest of all time. After his dad's murder in North Carolina, Michael Jordan spent years trying to understand what had happened and dealing with his depression. Finally, after several years of trying many other things, Michael returned to the one thing that was always a rewarding constant in his life—basketball. Through the lens of basketball, Michael Jordon rebuilt his world and life with competitiveness, grit, and determination to be in the of greatest of all time.

Donald Trump: The world is clear on where they stand on Donald Trump! You either love him or hate him, but you always hear him even if you tune him out. From his business career with many successes and failures, he turned his brand into a hugely successful TV series, earning over $60 million dollars per year. Then, when the odds were against him in every way, with fifteen professional politicians against him in the primary, he beat them all to become the Republican candidate for president of the United States. Facing the biggest political machine of all time, the Clintons, he beat the improbable odds to be elected president of the United States and the most powerful man in the free world. Setting aside all the conversation about the border with Mexico, all the noise around gas and oil, and every other controversy, Mr. Trump's legacy will be defined by one of the greatest acts of all time—saving the world. For the first time ever, the world was faced with the deadly pandemic of COVID-19. There was no precedent for this politically, economically and the devastating health effects of this pandemic?

While many aspects about the ultimate handling of the pandemic can be criticized, the one thing that cannot is the fact that Mr. Trump worked with the FDA and government agencies to help make the COVID-19 vaccine available to Americans at record speed and to fend off the possibility of millions more deaths. People love to Monday-morning quarterback these events, but when you are in the thick of things and people are dying every day, you must make extremely hard crisis-management decisions in the moment.

Trump made the improbable journey from businessperson to TV entertainer to president. Facing the greatest health and financial challenge of all time, Mr. Trump not only had to deal with the health consequences of COVID-19, but also the tremendous financial fallout as the country shut down for over a year. This devastated the economy and forced the federal government to create programs and liquidity for everyone.

The greatest comeback story of all time is Tiger Woods. Throughout his career, Tiger Woods had multiple back and knee surgeries. He managed to come back from all of his physical ailments at age forty-four to win the 2019 Masters Tournament, the most famous golf tournament in the world.

Tiger also faced multiple personal and financial difficulties. After his affairs came to light, Tiger had to endure the 24/7 news cycle of his liaisons with over 120 women, many of them coming out to try and extort a payday from Tiger for silence. Due to this scandal, all of his sponsors withdrew their endorsements under the morals clause in his contract. To make matters worse, Tiger was then arrested on DUI charges when he was found asleep at the wheel of his Mercedes on the side of the road late one night.

Finally, racing to an interview in California, Tiger's Genesis SUV flipped over on a winding curve and crashed into a tree in a single-car accident. Tiger had to be pulled out of the truck through the windshield and raced to a local hospital where they put pins and rods in his shattered leg and ankle. At one point, they considered amputating the leg due to the injury.

It is now fourteen months later as I am watching the 2022 Masters Tournament with a forty-six-year-old Tiger back from the dead, once again competing on the world stage.

What do all the above people have in common? Unstoppable determination and the will not to give up no matter the odds. So many times, when people face catastrophic consequences, they blame the world, give up, and pack it in for life. Not these winners. They recognized that they were winners before and can be winners again. With absolute superhuman effort, they dusted themselves off to make it back to the top.

After failure, you are in a bad place mentally. Failure takes a little while to occur. For that very reason, new success may take a little while to occur. The most important thing is to seek help in the form of conversation with a psychiatrist, a best friend, a brother, sister, or a parent. The people who had your back when you were on the top of the world are the very same people who hopefully have your back when you are the bottom. These people had a front-row seat to your world; they may see things that you are missing and help you on the road back.

The question is do these greats have a common mental illness in their genes that allow them to be so great, create chaos in their life through depression or plain mental illness of addiction or disease and then rebuild their life to a new height. Look at all the examples on this page. There is greatness, there is a setback, and then there is greatness again. What makes their storylines so perfect is that their struggles not only define their greatness but also beautify the fact that they are human. People cannot relate to the greatness, but they certainly can relate to the setbacks and the comebacks. This is what makes these comeback stories so relatable. Everyone knows someone who struggles with mental illness, depression, and addictions. Many of the people in our family have been touched with this. We are blessed to live in a society that has so much to offer in the way of help for all these problems.

CHAPTER 12
What Is in a Name?

Do you remember a TV show called *Gilligan's Island*? Well, there was a very wealthy couple stuck on an island, and the man's name was Thurston Howell III. Somehow with a name like that you knew what the character was all about before you even met him. The immediate assumption was that Thurston Howell III was some wealthy blue-blood guy and—guess what?—you are correct.

Bookstores are full of books about coming up with names for newborns. It is so much fun to pick a name for a new baby, but it's also particularly important because that is how that person will be identified their entire life. In the TV show Seinfeld, George wants to name his child "7" because it was Mickey Mantle's number on his jersey. George, for selfish reasons, wanted to name the child for his own purposes rather than considering how it would impact this child in school and later in life. A child's name should exude confidence; it should make a person feel good about what they call themselves.

What is in a name? A lot. In business, it is important to have a name that will be easy to say, that exudes class, and that in some way represents the business being promoted. I am not saying one thing has anything to do with another, but I remember back in the day we were dealing with a bank called First Union. At the time, First Union had been acquired by Wachovia Bank. For at least six months, everyone in my office had trouble saying Wachovia or writing Wachovia Bank; it seemed like it was an effort to say the name and feel comfortable with it. Did it chase people away from staying with this bank? Maybe. Did it make people not want to switch over to this bank? Maybe. Did it cause employees consternation with their job because of the name of this bank? Maybe. The bottom line is that it was an unnecessary obstacle to doing and retaining new business because the name was hard to say and write. Oddly enough, we all know now that Wachovia Bank failed and went out of business. Was it because of the name? No, but did the odd shape of the name have something to do with the business failing? My bet is yes. Was it 50% the cause, no, but it might have been 5% or 3% or 8%. It was something, as it was not a user-friendly experience?

One of the first things to do when creating a business from the start is to produce a name and a logo. Most business owners are narcissistic; they love to see their name in neon lights and often name the company after themselves. I can tell you from personal experience that this is a bad idea. First and foremost, if you are successful people will start to come after you because you have now become a public figure. If there are positive articles written about your business and it is your name, you win. Truth be told, for every good article there are two or more bad articles about your business, and this paints you in a negative light. Now, this is your name on the line. If you sell your business, then it becomes even more challenging because anything the new company does with your name creates conflict. What happens if this new company gets involved in shady business deal or even fraud? When articles are written about it, everyone thinks it is you. Not fun! The issue is to create something that will stand the test of time. What you want at the beginning of your business life, you may not want or need in the middle of your business life. Try and keep it simple.

Create a name that has meaning for what the product is that you are selling and promoting.

Consider some of the great companies and their names, and use this as a road map for ideas. For example, Apple Inc. has a great name that segues into a great logo. Or how about IBM, which is short for International Business Machines? No one wants to spit out those long words, but the acronym IBM is easy and fun to say. What about Dollar Tree or Five Below? Those names are perfect because they tell you exactly what the companies are about. The bottom line is this. Creating a great name helps create immediate buzz for what you are doing and trying to express. The more complicated the name, the harder it is to promote your message.

CHAPTER 13
Never Take Friendship for Granted

Besides a spouse or a significant other, friendship is so important in life. Life throws curveballs at you all the time, and having good friends helps smooth out the lumps in life.

I often ask people, "How many good friends do you have?" I call these the "3:30 a.m." people. If you have a problem, you can call them on the phone and they will come and meet you at 3:30 a.m., no questions asked. If you can count three or four of them, then you are a lucky person. You ask many people "How many friends do you have?" And they will say fifty. No one has fifty good friends, people who you can really count on when you need help or advice.

I love to study people and find the entire concept of friendship interesting. If you sit in a restaurant and look around the room, you may see various people in relationships and wonder how they came to be. Take for example two couples seated at a table and eating dinner. Let us say that these two couples belong to the same church or, for that matter, country club. There are tons of couples at these types of venues. How did these two couples become friends? People always have groups. For example, people play golf at a golf club with the same four or five people every week. How did they become friends? Single girls may go out together on a Friday or Saturday night. How did they all become friends? Sometimes you look at a group and they look the same: the guys are all bald or tall, the girls are all blondes, or they are all heavy. Some friendships have a "jealous factor." It is funny—we used to call that friend enemies. That is an enemy who acts like a friend and is friendly to your face but who secretly hopes that you will fail.

While there a few (very few) friendships where you can be completely honest and open, it is the fragility of friendship that amazes me. You could be friends with someone for fifteen years, but if their spouse makes an inappropriate comment then the entire friendship may come unglued. That's fifteen years of friendship wiped away in minutes. Do we lack the tools to put humpy-dumpty back together again, or are we too lazy to try and figure it is not worth it? If a friendship is meaningful and real, you will find the skills to put it back together again. If the relationship is too much work or just a veneer, then let it fall apart or transition into more casual relationship (which may not be a terrible thing).

Life is tough, and everyone needs a sounding board. If you are lucky enough to have those three or four friends who are close and special, cherish those relationships. If you hit some bumps along the way, work hard to smooth them out, even if doing so requires an apology. As we know, most people hate to apologize or admit they are wrong. Sometimes to save a worthwhile relationship, you will need to apologize even if you feel you are right. In many instances, both parties are a little bit wrong, and both will need to step up and do the right thing—say the right words to make the problem disappear. Even if you feel you were partially right and the other side will not bend, if you value the friendship then it might be worth it to put your ego away and make it right. This is the hardest thing to do. If the friend is a true best friend, they will understand this and do the same. Unfortunately, some people do not have the capacity to do this. In this case, be the bigger person. Bury your ego to save the friendship.

For over thirty years, I had one of those special kind of friendship with a guy. We would talk on the phone at least three or four times a day. It was great. We would call each other and talk about our day or what we were having for lunch or dinner. Many phone calls were like "And what did you have for lunch today? What did you have for a snack today?" And, and, and. Just silly talk. At one point we started running the boardwalk in Atlantic City together, running from one end to the other. When we made it the five miles to the end, we would take a cab back to our starting point and laugh all the way. This only lasted one summer, but it was a wonderful experience.

Then my friend moved up to the Hamptons for the summer. I sold my house on the Jersey Shore and moved up there as well. We would have the most fantastic barbecues with all the kids on the weekends. My friend was the barbecue maestro; we used to joke that when we cooked steaks, he would put twelve steaks on the barbecue and ten would come off because he had to taste-test them while cooking.

Long story short, after my last divorce, his wife took a side, and it was not my side. The sad part of a divorce (besides the kids and the money) is who gets custody of the friends and friendships. Initially, it does not work that the friends you had as a couple immediately become friends when you are single. Obviously, the other couple is not going to put their relationship at risk fighting over who broke up and who maintains that friendship. Suffice to say that it was difficult for all four of us. Bottom line: My best friend and I did not talk for years. It was extremely difficult; every morning I missed those calls to talk about nothing and the same during the night.

So, what happened? My ex and I eventually became friendly again after the separation. We had an amazing child together and at some point both realized that life is easier when we get along rather than fight. As that relationship improved, it opened the door for my best friend and I to start talking again. Like anything else, it started out slow, but within a few months it was back where it used to be. Now we talk three or four times a day, and it is great. I am so happy it worked out because my life is better with him in it.

The point of the story is that important friendships are more valuable than fights or break-ups. In my case, there was much more to our friendship on a personal level than the one issue that broke us apart. It took years for both of us to see that and to realize that we were missing out sharing our lives together as we grew older. I am incredibly grateful that we worked it out; if we had not, we would have both missed a great friendship for the rest of our lives. Is there a scar there? Sure. But the bleeding has stopped, and we are back to having fun again.

CHAPTER 14
The Most Important Meal of the Day

Lunch is the most important meal of the day, and this is true for several reasons. First, lunch gives you good nutrition at the middle of the day. It's the energy you need to plow your way through the rest of the day. Many people skip breakfast and have a cup of coffee instead, so their first real meal is lunch. While skipping breakfast is a bad idea, even a light breakfast does not give you the energy your body craves to tackle problems head on.

Second, lunch is the very excuse to regroup during the day. Often, when the day starts there are pent-up problems from the day before, or people on the phones who are immediately looking for a resolution. Sometimes, these people have "stewed" all night and cannot wait to jump on you first thing in the morning. Then of course there is your routine in the morning, whatever that may be...working out...paying bills...getting organize at your desk for your workday, then boom you are off and on your way.

The reason lunch is such a great aspect of the day is simple. It is a break in the action, much like half-time in sports. In the business world, this gives you a set time of the day to stand up from your desk, walk away from what you are working on, and regroup. Many times during the day, you cannot see the forest for the trees because you are rushed and overwhelmed with problems. The simple break of briefly walking away from your work, getting some fuel and some fun conversation, gives you a chance to go back to your day with a fresh attitude and the mindset to tackle problems with a more measured approach.

There are many people who say, "I work through lunch." That is just stupid. Take a friggin' half hour to regroup and stay an extra half hour at the end of the day, if you need the extra time. Your body and mind cannot run like a car without maintenance. This half-time break gives you and your work what it needs for the balance of the day—for your attention span to be at its highest level and for your energy and thought process to be sharp.

On a personal level, it gives you a chance to get away from work and to make your personal calls to your wife, girlfriend, or kids and to give them some undivided attention. Many times, when you are sitting at your desk working, you're half in and half out of a conversation with friends or family. You are not giving a fair response to their conversation because your mind is not with them; it is at work or whatever you are doing. A lunch break gives you undivided attention to have some fun, be serious, or to better deal with personal issues one-on-one. You will be amazed how coming back from lunch refreshed gives you a better approach moving forward.

I get up from my desk, get in my car (which is a pain in the ass), and drive a few miles to a great lunch spot that has hot fresh food. There are always people in there to chat with and have a few laughs before returning to work. After lunch, I get into my car and drive the short distance back to work while listening to the radio or making a few phone calls. As I pull into the parking lot and get out of my car, I feel like a new person with a much better attitude than when I left

Many people take lunch meetings, which is always a great idea. It gives you a much more casual approach to discussing business, and you can get to know your associate a little better. In this way, it becomes possible to build relationships or friendships through lunching together, which can help you resolve one-on-one issues more efficiently. In all the bank meetings that I have had in my career, after the blizzard of paperwork on the conference table was resolved or signed, there was always a nice lunch to build on what we had accomplished. People discount this concept as a waste of time; I view it as an energy builder, a regrouping stage of the day to come back at your problems and issues with a fresh new attitude.

CHAPTER 15
Disappointment and Its Many Forms

Everyone experiences disappointment, and everyone deals with it in different ways. Disappointment can come in work (getting a job, keeping a job), friendship, and family. Disappointment can come in relationships, whether starting, ending, or somewhere in between. The bottom line is that disappointment can have a different face every time.

When someone is disappointed, there may also be feelings of depression associated with the disappointment. Yet disappointment can be one of the most motivating things that can happen to a person. From disappointment, we learn lessons that help us cope with similar situations. These lessons ensure that we do not repeatedly put ourselves in a position where we "set ourselves up" for the same disappointment. It toughens us up so that the next time it is not as big a blow. It makes us realize that others are not you, and because others are not you the expectation level must be tempered not in terms of what you expect, which can always be high, but instead the rationalization of the outcome if it does not meet your standard. Bottom line is how do you deal with disappointment and rationalize it.

One example is when you meet someone new with the prospect of starting a new relationship. Relationships are as old as time, and everyone wants to be in one. Say for example that I meet someone new. I really like this person, so I call, I text, and I set up a date. The

Disappointment and Its Many Forms

first date goes well. The next time I call or text, the response time is slower and then slower. What is going on? I really like this person and thought the first date was amazing. I took her out to a fantastic restaurant, we drank, we ate, and we laughed. Why are the phone calls going straight to voicemail and the texts are being returned in twelve hours instead of twelve minutes? My expectations could be tempered, and my disappointment alleviated, if the other party sent a straightforward text or phone call that explained that I was not their type, or vice versa, rather than "ghosting" me. If you had envisioned yourself in a relationship with this other person then this is true disappointment. The trick is how to deal with and recover from it. Certainly, the first time it happens is hard. The second and third time, it gets easier; you know the signs when things are going south.

Why is an example like the above a true motivating factor in life? Simple: You learn. You get stronger and tougher, and you learn how to control your emotions good or bad. You get to dust yourself off, get up off the emotional ground, and move forward. Would the disappointment be easier if there was an explanation? Sure. But there is not one, so deal with it. Their reaction is the same, explanation or not—no relationship. Could you continue to try different things to move the relationship along? Sure. But you are better off moving on and trying again in six months with a fresh approach. By then maybe the other individual will be in a better place or ready to accept you differently.

Disappointment shows up in many places and forms. It is not one of life's great feelings. In fact, it sucks. Time is spent rationalizing what happened, but then the issue must be put to bed. You cannot spend an inordinate amount of time dwelling on the issue. Move on, find some thoughts that bring you joy, and get out of the funk of dealing with disappoint. In the above example, this person is not going to go out with me again, so I must move on and find someone else, plain and simple. Sitting here, looking at her picture, and feeling sorry for myself is not going to get me another date. At the end of the day, it is the best thing that could happen, because I will find someone better for me.

Another example is when one of your projects or jobs fails. That is a horrible feeling. Of course, you can continue to try and turn things around, but at some point you realize that the job or project is not going to work out. Making the assessment of spending your time in a positive way versus a negative way is particularly important. Remember: Time is your most valuable asset. Do not waste it, because it is the one thing you can never get back. There is disappointment, but you cannot dwell on it—learn from it. Take this experience and try to avoid repeating the things that created this disappointment. This is an extremely challenging thing to do because we are all human beings and do not want to admit our real disappointments.

CHAPTER 16
One Step at a Time

When you are faced with adversity in life and problems seem insurmountable, take a step back and remember the adage, "One step at a time." It's an expression that has held true in every problem that I have tried to solve in my business and personal career.

Most problems have multiple tiers that affect each other. It is impossible to attack the entire problem all at once for several reasons. First, as you solve part of a problem, another solution may come up to solve more of the problem. The bottom line is you need to pick one spot and start there. Work your way down and through the other problems until you come to the ultimate solution one step at a time. As you start to solve the problem piece-by-piece, the remaining pieces become easier to solve because they are no longer as important to the overall issue. The resolution may be easier now that other things are in place.

Take, for example, a divorce. Wow, there are a ton of issues: child custody and child support, monetary settlements, custody of the house/cars/china and whatever else the couple owned and shared, a business, if you have one. Then, finally, who gets custody of the friends. Everything will fall into place if you go slow. If you try and race through the process, it will be a disaster.

The most important issue to work on first is with any kids—who has them and what amount of time each person gets to see them. This is always tricky because kids are usually terribly upset by a divorce, often blaming one party or another. If you can be civil and work that out first, that is huge positive step in the right direction.

The second important issue is that you must understand the law. You may not like the law, you may not agree with the law, but in order for you to stay sane, you should understand what your rights are and what your spouse's rights are. If you do not like the landscape, suck it up and go back with your husband or wife. If you are not happy, you have to understand what the law will provide for you and accept those facts. You can certainly challenge everything and may save a few pennies, but in the end the lawyers will get rich and it will cost you the same amount of money except with bad will and aggravation.

As you get through these two issues, you will realize that, unless they are family heirlooms, physical belongings hold extraordinarily little value in a long life. So, when you move into your new place and you have two TVs instead of five, big deal. You will rebuild. What you get or take with you is so minor that it is not worth fighting about.

Now, when it comes to custody of friends, that is a hard one. In my experience, it just falls into place. Over time, you will probably have friends on both "sides." In the short term, it feels raw; everyone picks a corner and starts swinging for their favorite. But ten years later, no one really cares.

Over the past two weeks, I have had the most incredible experience. My son graduated the University of Pennsylvania, and the entire weekend was full of frat parties, graduation ceremonies, and dinners big and small. My second wife and I had the worst and most contentious divorce in the world. It was horrible, with the two lawyers battling it out on every front. At the time, my wife was a famous TV news anchor, so every court filing by her was in the press. It was embarrassing and humiliating. (In fact, our divorce was on the cover of the local newspaper numerous times.)

Guess what? That was nineteen years ago, and our son is graduating from the best business school in the country as an economics major. He was hired by a Wall Street bank as an investment banker and is happy. Both my ex-wife and I had little contact over the past ten years, but we went to this graduation with huge smiles on our faces, enjoyed dinners and parties together, and celebrated our son's success. It took his success, and separate time away from each other, to heal all wounds. Are we going to contact each other and chat? No, but it now sets the standard for future events that life with our son brings, such as marriage or having a child. We are both inexplicably bound by this successful young man, so we manage to keep our egos in check and promote his happiness.

The lesson learned was simple: One step at a time. The hard stuff happens in the beginning, and over time the other stuff manages to work itself out by fading away. There always must be a self-diagnosis to assess what is important and what is complete nonsense. What was really important was my son, his accomplishment, and his friends and the camaraderie of his frat brothers. What was unimportant was my ex-wife and our petty differences that are now meaningless. So much time has passed, and both our lives have moved on with many new and different experiences. The process was difficult, but if you take one step at a time, then the remaining issues to resolve get smaller and smaller until you are done.

It's like building a house. You start by clearing the ground. Then you stake out the foundation, dig the hole, and put the foundation in.

One Step at a Time

As you start to frame the house, you put in the plumbing, the heating and air conditioning, the electrical, and so on. Step by step, you have a completed house. One stage does not happen before another because it cannot; every stage needs the one that came before it to complete the project.

Everything in life is step by step. Making a delicious dinner starts with buying the ingredients, then preparing the meat or the salad. Each step requires getting the ingredients together in their raw form and following more steps to make them into the finish product.

I find that as I have gotten older, it is easier to go slow and take it one step at a time to complete any project, whether preparing a meal, painting a room, or starting a diet. If I go slow, then the end is much quicker because I do not make mistakes. That old expression is so true: I never have time to do it right, but I always have time to do it over!

Take your time, take one step at a time, and you will complete your goal in the quickest, most efficient way.

CHAPTER 17

The Meaning of Respect in Business and in Life

In business, respect is one of the most important words. People discount respect because of their egos! Sure, having an ego in business is particularly important, but so is having respect of others. It makes you a better person and a great leader. Respect in your personal life is equally important. Respecting your family, your friends, your business associates, even the mail carrier and the police officer is an everyday occurrence. It makes you feel better as a person, and it makes others feel great as well.

Years ago, I entered a business deal with a commercial real estate developer. The deal was that the developer would buy the property and subdivide it; he would keep the office buildings, and I would use the remaining property to build residential houses. The developer was going to get a bank loan to buy the property. Once he had it subdivided between the commercial property and the residential property, I would then settle and pay the developer for the residential portion. It would take several years to make all that zoning happen.

That is not what happened. As the developer was trying to secure financing, I received a call from his banker. Let us say his name was Chris. Chris tells me that he needs my financial statement for the loan. I explained to Chris repeatedly that he did not understand the deal. I

The Meaning of Respect in Business and in Life

was not borrowing money from him with my partner; the deal called for me to close on the ground over the year as my partner was able to obtain the approvals. It was the developer's responsibility to buy the ground first and get the approvals.

After I tried hard to explain this to Chris, I regretfully lost my cool. I disrespected this banker by saying things that were not appropriate. At the time, I was the largest privately held builder in the Delaware Valley, very full of myself, and obviously felt the liberty to abuse this banker. Chris hated me for the way I responded to his request for financial statements. At the end of the day, and for other reasons, the deal never went through as originally intended. We found a buyer right away and flipped the property never having to settle on it.

Years later, I had a loan on thousands of acres of vacant ground with a wonderful bank that had been in business for fifty-five years. As with most older banks, the founder died, and the bank was sold to a much larger bank. Land loans were almost impossible to obtain because land costs money (real estate taxes) and yields no income until it is sold. For these reasons, banks really do not want to lend against raw ground.

You know where this is headed. Years later, my secretary buzzes me and says some banker named Chris is on the phone. He is the head of the bank that just bought the smaller bank with which I had a land loan. Hoping it was a different Chris, I picked up the phone and starting speaking. On the other end of the phone was the same Chris that, years earlier, I had "ripped" for not giving him and his bank my financials. He precedes to tell me his bank is now my new lender. He was reviewing my loan, and it did not meet the criteria for the type of lending they are doing. I needed six months to find a new lender to pay off his bank. I reluctantly accepted this because I knew I had a huge conflict with this guy, who was now the president of the bank that owned my loan. Chris then reminded me of our heated conversation years prior and basically said, "Life is a bitch. You will have to figure it out." I had thirty days to pay off my loan to his bank, not the six months I requested.

Years earlier, if I had given Chris the proper respect, I could have helped him out doing the paperwork on the loan and helped myself out by making a new friend and a future banker. I could kick myself for having been such an asshole. Chris was not asking me to cosign a loan; all he was asking for was stuff to put in his file (or a file stuffer as it is called in the banking industry). Instead of giving it to him, I was an arrogant asshole, and I paid the price years later. I ended up getting another, more expensive loan with more equity required, but not until long after this loan expired, which caused me tremendous grief and aggravation with lawsuits and lawyers. All of which were unnecessary if I had only worked with Chris's request years ago.

There's an old expression: "The same people you meet on the elevator ride up are the same people you meet on the elevator ride down." I was a big shot when I told Chris to go to hell. When the tide—and the economy—turned, it sure would have been nice to have Chris in my corner to renew my loans. That was not going to happen because of my attitude. It was a pain in the ass, but we worked through it, although it was completely unnecessary. It would have been just as easy to have gone along with Chris and give him the information he requested, but I needed to show him he was screwing with the wrong guy. Guess what? It turns out I was the one screwing with the wrong guy, as I would later find out. I did not have any respect for Chris because I did not understand or want to give him what he needed. I did not respect his position, not realizing that he was young and so was

I and that, in our community, I would someday run into him later in life. I was wrong, and I paid the price.

This was a valuable lesson, and hopefully I will never repeat it. If I had asked the proper questions and considered Chris's request and assurances, I would have never had this conflict. Looking back on the experience, I made a mistake. I did not give Chris my financial information for his file, so I created bad will and would never do business with him. After the fact Chris did not extend my loan and if circumstances changed in the future, I would not do business with him. The overall problem was that after it was all finished and I replaced the loan, I should have put my animosity aside and called Chris, met him for lunch, and buried that hatchet so that we could have been business friends and worked together in future. As an older man, I would know to do that as I younger man I was too angry to understand the world is round. I hope if you are reading this book, you learn a lesson from my stupid mistakes and bad experiences.

CHAPTER 18
Speak So That People Will Understand

In life, you will do better if you speak plainly rather than in long-winded nonsense. Just tell it the way it is, and you will always remember what you said. Lies or double talk are difficult to remember, and you will always get caught. If you project where you are going and let people know the path forward, then they can never be disappointed, only happy because the way forward will either be projected to manage expectations or exceed those expectations.

If you speak plain language, it is easy to manage expectation. Too many people paint unrealistic rosy pictures rather than trying to manage the conversation in a realistic light, leaving upside as a benefit.

I've been married several times and have four kids. Dating is always a challenge. When asked "Have you ever been married before?" I come right out and say, "Yes, three times!" Usually, you can see "how do I get out of here?" on your date's face, but I manage their expectation and tell them the truth. My first marriage was when I was young. My second marriage was to a famous person, which is fun but not normal. In the third marriage, it was difficult trying to put the pieces together in a harmonious way—blending four kids from three different mothers. Then I explain that my future focus is to make my kids a family, not half-brothers or half-sisters but a unit that is impenetrable. This requires constant communication and honesty.

Speak So That People Will Understand

Ultimately, if you speak plainly and respond honestly, you can explain your position. While some people may not agree with it or like your lifestyle, they will respect you for managing it as a stand-up person and for being realistic about the mess you made and how you intend to make things right. If you're on a date, they may either never want see you again (which rarely happens, ha-ha) or they might think, "Okay, let me see where this road takes me. This guy is nuts, but there is something here we can work with because at least he sees what his past looks like and is trying to make his future a better place. At a minimum, I will have a nice dinner and conversation and go home and go to sleep."

One of the greatest plain-language conversations you can have is about driving. Have you ever noticed that drivers always look forward? When they are looking for a street or a parking spot or looking at someone on the side of the road, no one—I repeat, no one—looks in their review mirror unless their rear car camera is beeping. The greatest part of life is the rear view! It is your history. It is your knowledge that helps you navigate the future in a more desirous way. You know what you like, you know right from wrong, and you know how to navigate the potholes of life. The rear view is so important, and no one wants to look in it. Think about it and use it.

A remarkably simple example is playing golf. Let us assume that you are playing an incredibly challenging course. Is it easier the second and then third time you play it. The course will still be challenging, but now you have the knowledge of where to hit the ball and what each hole looks like. This is the same as looking in the rear-view mirror of life. You know how it turned out in the past, so use it to your advantage for the future.

I watched a great interview with Michael Milken, the junk bond king, and David Rubenstein, a billionaire investor who happens to stream interviews of famous wealthy people. In creating the financial vehicle called the junk bond, there were lines that were crossed. This caused the government to come after Milken and to put him in jail for several years for certain financial crimes.

Michael Milken may arguably be one of the smartest guys to graduate from the University of Pennsylvania. He had the highest-recorded grades in the school's history and is a huge thinker as a result of his schooling, career, and life experiences. He was diagnosed with advanced stage-four prostate cancer. His response upon hearing this death sentence was to lie on the ground in silence and think about his life for twenty-four hours in the rear-view mirror and try and produce a plan to not only survive but to live. Milken relied on his life experience to look back to look forward to surviving. He produced a very unconventional plan for his recovery (not unlike his invention of the junk bond). It was bold, it was out of the box, and it worked! Not only did he survive, he has been in remission for over twenty years and doing fantastic at age seventy-four. The positive of Michael's story is what amazing things he is doing for medicine and others because of his good luck and second chance on life. This amazing guy is thankful for a second chance and wants to make sure he helps others have the same luck he has had.

The rear-view mirror is a replica of a better future. You cannot change it, but you can use it to change the future. Use plain language in explaining your plan so you can manage expectations even if you are extremely optimistic about the future. If you are a leader, you must do exactly that... Lead people in a positive direction to a good future. Use the past to explain the future.

Montgomery Walk 55 plus community

Back of a community Clubhouse

Back of a Clubhouse for a 500 unit community

Logo for Cutty and Govy Podcast

Speak So That People Will Understand

Estate model home

CHAPTER 19
Humility Is Motivation

Back in the day, being the largest privately held builder in the market had many ups and many downs. One thing that I loved to do was to motivate people through action. At the time, we had twenty-five developments of one hundred homes or more with at least 250 houses under construction at any given point. This required a huge work force of 5,000 people working for our company who were paid weekly. I knew a few of the old-time guys, but most of the people I did not know.

My work was always an office job, but once or twice a week I would visit some of my communities to see how the construction was going. I loved this part of my job. I would do this on the way back to my office after lunch. Most of my career, I drove some fancy exotic car, and when I pulled up to a job site, the guys knew I was there. All the crap stopped, and they were all business.

There were three things I always did to motivate people. First, I would walk into a couple of the houses under construction. Usually there was a laborer in the house sweeping or moving supplies around. I would go up to this person and introduce myself; they were usually nervous. I would ask them about their job, what they did, and if they had any advice for me. Usually, they looked at me dumbfounded. They wanted to know why this guy in a fancy suit, the owner of all this, would want advice from a laborer. Usually, they were very honored and would go on to tell me about their world. They would walk me out to the dumpster, which was placed on every lot under construction and say, "Look here, Mr. C. Do you see what I am throwing out every day? There are bags of sand, huge pieces of lumber, drywall, pieces of millwork, kitchen cabinets..." The laborer would then teach me a giant lesson. "Mr. C," he said, "always go to the dumpster on every lot, and you will see all the mistakes for which you are paying. Your project manager will never tell you, because they are his mistakes. I have nothing to lose by telling you." What did I learn from the lowest-paid guy on that job site? I learned that the lowest-paid guy would make me the most money because he sees it and lives it. He is proud of his job but realizes that his bosses know what is going on and if he rats them out, he will get fired. The laborer is in survival mode.

The second remarkable thing is to walk around with the project manager and learn his view on the community. As I did this, he would whisper to me the name of the plumber or electrician who we were approaching. I would walk up to the plumber and say, "How you are doing, Bobby?" The plumber would be astonished that I knew his name and cared enough to walk up and say hello. Spending time with this guy was such an important part of my visit. I learned how we could do a better job and thanked him for all his demanding work. If I gave the guy $500, he would not be as happy as by the simple respect I showed him. Trust me, he went home that night and felt like a five-hundred-pound gorilla telling his wife and kids how he schooled the boss and how every word he said was listened to and appreciated. This act of kindness and respect cost me nothing, but the rewards were plentiful. Furthermore, the most underutilized tool for motivation is the use of someone's name. I love it when people address me by name. It means they care enough about their interactions with me to remember my name and use it.

Finally, the crazy stuff. We always had to build crazy roads and infrastructure before we could start building houses; there was nothing but mud everywhere. I would pull onto a job site and look thousands of yards away to see a giant backhoe putting pipe in the ground. I always had mud shoes in the trunk of my car. I would start driving my fancy, exotic car out to the guys putting the pipe in the ground. As I approached the pipe crew, I could hear the big backhoe shutting down so they could talk to me. I could see the expressions on their faces, thinking "Who is this crazy motherf*er, destroying a fancy car by driving across a field of mud?"

I would get out of my car and say, "Hey, guys, how is it going?" I'd look into the trench, not know what the hell I was looking at. They would say, "Mr. C, how could you drive such a gorgeous car across that mud and take a chance of ruining it?" My response was they are making tons of these cars. "I can always get it repaired or buy another one of them. It is more important for me to come out here, shake your hands, and thank you for your demanding work than worry about a stupid car." They all would look at me astonished but determined to work harder, safer, and better. They understood that I respected their efforts; they in turn were determined to do the best job they could.

I would chat with them for about ten or fifteen minutes, laughing and joking about life. If the coffee truck pulled up, I would say, "It's on me today." The guys would grab two or three sandwiches, sodas, and coffee, probably thinking, "The boss is paying. Let us get what we can." The coffee girl would always turn nervously to me as she added up the tab and say, "Mr. C, it is $126!" I would happily pull out the money and pay with a big smile.

Humility Is Motivation

Again, true motivation. These guys were doing demanding work. They earned and deserved my respect for the hard and dangerous work they were doing. I accepted the responsibility with humility and respect. Two groups were happy: The guys felt respected and appreciated, and I felt the same way.

CHAPTER 20
Accomplished by 7:30 a.m.

Scheduling your day is particularly important to the organization of your life. For example, I am an early riser. In the morning, I wake up at 5 a.m., make the bed, wash my face, brush my teeth, put on my gym clothes, and go downstairs. I eat a banana, drink some green juice, then get in my car to drive to Starbucks for morning coffee. After I get my coffee, I walk across the street to buy my newspapers at the local 7-Eleven. Back in the car, it's off to the gym at 5:30 a.m. where I work out hard for an hour. Across the street from the gym is another Starbucks, where I order an iced tea and add vitamin C powder to help prevent colds and keep away all the boogeymen. It works.

I pull out of the lot and drive up the street to the supermarket where I buy bananas, green juice, and a few things to last the next few days. (I am in the supermarket at least two times a week.) Afterward, I drive about a mile to the bank to get some cash out of the ATM machine. Back in the car, it's off to the gas station to gas up my car. My final stop is a bagel store with a stone-fired wood stove for a deliciously fresh bagel. Back in the car and I return home, pull into my driveway, and go inside to turn on the stock channel. I sit down and start to eat my bagel, drink some water, and read the newspapers I bought that morning. As I look at my watch, I see that it is only 7:30 a.m.Look at what I have accomplished, and it is only 7:30 a.m. And I haven't even begun my business day. When you organize your day, you can get the most done in the brief time that you have. I work all day and really do not leave my office except for lunch. It is important to get the most done in the morning because the evening is my downtime to relax. The secret of my morning routine is that I plan my route ahead of time so that I don't drive too far. Pick the one thing that is mandatory to do every day—for me, it is the gym. The remaining items in my morning routine must revolve around the gym and be nearby. In most cities, the big gyms are all near the other places that I visit, like a Starbucks or a place to get newspapers or cash at a ATM. Now I have a road map of my route that is all within several miles of my gym. All of these places are open early, so I can get everything done in one trip and be back at my office by 7:30 a.m.

Writing this stuff down is also important. Write down on a piece of paper all of the things that you want to do in a day then stare at the list and organize it in order of priority and efficiency. For example, if you are working on your finances, something as simple as having your checkbook and a calculator out and the folders you need open can save you a huge amount of time. (It avoids taking stuff out of drawers, putting them back into drawers, then taking them out again.) Try to do one project at a time and complete that project first rather than jumping around and doing several things at once.

Once again, writing stuff down is important. I hate it when I go into a restaurant and the server tries to impress you by taking the food order of six people without writing anything down. I understand that some waitstaff are exceptionally good at their jobs and are trained to do this, but it is complete bullshit. One person might have a salad with no blue cheese crumbles, a baked potato (dry, no sides), a medium-rare steak, an iced tea (no lemon); the other five people will have the same type of order but with all kinds of changes to the menu items. If the server writes nothing down, then what are the chances that this order for six people will come out perfect? (Unless this server won the server of the year contest.) It can be painful when five people get their food, but the sixth person's food is screwed up and must be sent back. This is awkward and hard to deal with, and the same is true for your workday. Write down your tasks and your thoughts (or have someone do so for you) so that the chances of missing anything or making mistakes is minimal.

Even writing down random thoughts is great. Everyone carries their cell phone all the time now, and I have a spot on my phone where I save my random thoughts that I have while traveling throughout my day. When I have a chance later in the day, I look at the notes on my phone and write down my ideas for future reference.

Try to avoid meetings, especially big meetings with lots of people. Those meetings take too much time and accomplish extraordinarily little. If a meeting is required, sort out the agenda in advance; often, many of the issues can be resolved before the meeting. This limits the agenda to the important items that you are there to discuss and allows pinpoint accuracy to resolve those issues. (There's always someone in a meeting who wants to impress everyone with their brilliance or attention to detail, or the comedian who wants to make everyone laugh. Try to avoid that in meetings, as it is a huge waste of time.)

Phone calls are the most disruptive force in the day and can slow down your momentum. Unless I need a break or need to call someone for information, I do not take phone calls while I am working or sitting at my desk. It is too much of a waste of time. I personally try to save my phone calls for when I am driving (because driving is also a huge waste of time); if I can call my friends or my kids during a car ride, I kill two birds with one stone. (Unfortunately, no one is up as early as

I am when I go to the gym, so I wait until I go to lunch to make my phone calls on in the car.)

Finally, I try and plan the hard stuff for in the morning or early afternoon right after lunch and save the fun or easy stuff for the end of the day. When the fun stuff is at the end of the day, you get to end your day with a smile on your face. This is equally true for the easy stuff. The easy stuff allows you to glide into the day without too much of the stress that can keep you up all night long.

At the end of each day, I look back at my accomplishments and my failures. Hopefully, there are little-to-no failures and many accomplishments. There is also the list of uncompleted items, which again you hope you have completed everything unless it is a project that will take multiple days to complete. Obviously, if there are things that you did not get to that day, you need to put them on the top of your list for the next day.

The world is tough. If you are organized and find ways to save time, then you have an exceptionally good chance of being successful. Try to create a routine that allows everything to fall in place.

CHAPTER 21

Music and Its Special Place in Life

When you get into your car, go to the gym, cleaning your house, sitting on the beach or one of many other things music just allows you to be in a special place.

When I was young, there was always music playing on the radio (and it was often played through gigantic stereo systems in a dorm room or in your house.) Today, it is easy to listen to music on your phone, or to listen seamlessly through your ear buds. And there are so many other ways to listen to music: concerts, satellites services, Wi-Fi, Spotify, and on and on.

Let us start with a concert of your favorite entertainer or someone you like. Usually this takes place on a weekend when you are completely relaxed. I can honestly say that the concerts I choose to go to are usually particularly good. It has been a long time since I have seen a bad concert.

Music has a way of touching your brain cells that moves things around, like your taste buds do for food. When you hear good music, it makes you smile. You start to snap your fingers, move your legs, and shake your body to the beat. You feel good.

There are all kinds of music. There is music like the theme from Rocky that is great for sporting events. There is jazz music for when you are feeling mellow and want to relax. There are Barry White love ballads that are very sensual. There are rants and cheers for school sporting events. Rap music might make you smile or feel part of something greater. And crooners like Frank Sinatra or Dean Martin makes for smooth listening; it can be fun to fantasize about the good life they are singing about. You close your eyes and imaging life in the four corners in the song they are singing.

In the world of motivation, music sits at the top. Every month, I drag my sorry ass into the gym at 5:30 a.m. with a cup of coffee in one hand and my iPhone in the other. I get on the treadmill and start my playlist of music that I think will be useful for the day. By the time I am through the first song, I am in—I am rocking, shaking, and feeling good about working out and doing what I am doing.

Music can set the tone for a high school play or a Broadway show. As you take your seat, you feel the breeze from the air conditioning, watch the lights dim, and then—boom!—the orchestra begins. Now you are in the zone for a great show. Your attitude changes with each musical note that is played. This music set the anticipation of the show you are about to see and speaks a subliminal language that gets your body and brain in a great spot.

Of course, there is also music that you hate. Walk away and avoid listening to it, as it will put you in a bad mood. Who knows why we hate certain music? And who cares? There is such a vast selection of music that you can and should listen to; so, listen to what you want, whatever gets you motivated, and enjoy the music.

There is also mastering the art of playing a musical instrument, such as the piano or the guitar. This is a tremendous accomplishment, whether you play alone or in a band. My son was in a jazz band in high school, and I saw first the smile on his face when his band struck up a story and song and the band was cranking out these tunes. The head of the jazz band was an older guy with a bow tie named Mr. Fitzsimmons (or Fitz, as the class called him). Fitz would sit at the piano and pound the ivories, moving every part of his body from side to side, up and down, and all around to the music the jazz band was playing. It was infectious to say the least.

Music is a wonderful part of life. It is the ultimate aphrodisiac that allows you to reset the tone of your day or week and quickly gets you in a good headspace. There are so many aspects of music that create a wide playing field to enjoy the full body of the word. When you are feeling like you need a pick me up and some real motivation, turn to music. Play it in your car or see a show. Use it as a break or a time out to regroup.

CHAPTER 22

How to Recognize an Asshole

This is my favorite chapter in this book. We all know assholes. Everyone either has one in their life or has had firsthand experience with a real asshole. Assholes take all forms, shapes, and sizes. He could be a server, a bartender, or a banker. She could be a police officer (although I like the police), a coach, or an average person. Or someone who is so unrealistic that they fall into the asshole category.

The other night, I was sitting at the bar in a restaurant talking to the general manager when an asshole came up and wanted a piece of the general manager's ass! I had a front-row seat to this exchange, and to this day I have no idea what it was about. This was a wonderful steak house where everything is done right! Now, every seat in a restaurant is not the same. (The comedian Jackie Mason that had a skit about people saying that the seat "is too close to the door, too far from the window, a round table not square, too far back in the room, it is too quiet back there, it is too loud back there.") This sixty-year-old guy comes up to the general manager and starts tearing into him about where he is seated and how it is not the server he requested. Meanwhile, the general manager could not have been more accommodating, asking, "Is there something wrong with the service?" The answer: no. "Is there something wrong with table?" He says "It's too far away from the music and the center of the room where the energy is. And it happens to be my birthday."

The manager replies that he would be happy to move him when another table opens in about a half hour. At that, the asshole explodes, screaming that waiting a half hour is not acceptable. As I am watching this scene, I am trying to figure out what this restaurant and the manager did wrong. The restaurant has 220 seats. Some seats are great, some are okay, while other seats are not so great but still nice. Every table looks the same. The china is the same. The only difference is the location of any given table. Someone, usually a regular patron or an important person (big tipper, rich or famous, whatever that means) gets the great tables. The rest of the world gets the okay or not-so-okay tables. It is part of life. If the service and the food are good, then I can deal with where I sit. Would I like to be at a better table? Sure, but it is not the end of the world. But this asshole goes on and on that it is his birthday and he deserves better.

The scene reminds me of when I was young and I used to watch professional wrestling or WWE with Hulk Hogan. There was always a good guy and a bad guy in the match. Many times, the bad guy would win so there could be a rematch. At some point in the match, the bad guy knocks the good guy unconscious. The good guy is on the ground unconscious as the bad guy continues to pound away, kicking and punching the good guy while the referee tries to pull the bad guy off. That is what is happening here.

The manager says, "What can I do to make you happy? You say the food was good and the service was good." The asshole says it is his birthday and he did not like where he sat, so he wants a free meal. The manager quickly says he will send over a free desert. "No good," the asshole says in a loud voice. He wants a free dinner for him and his wife. Finally, after ten minutes of this beating, the manager relents and gives him a gift certificate for another evening. The asshole's response is that this is not good enough; he wants tonight's dinner paid for. The manager eventually gave in, but I give him all the credit in the world for keeping his cool. I would have thrown this guy out of the restaurant and banned him forever. Instead, the manager was nothing but professional and figured this happens at this extreme level occasionally so it is the cost of doing business.

As we move through life, we find these assholes at every level. My previous career was in homebuilding. I met many assholes along the way because they had power over me and they could be an asshole. For example, some building inspectors were nice, but many were assholes because they could be. Actually, this does not mean they are being tough; it means they are being a jerk. Let us say that you have a scheduled an inspection with a plumber and the building inspector at 1 p.m. The building inspector shows up at 5 p.m. after waiting all day and not getting any returns calls as to the status. Just because we were not there at 5 p.m. because the plumber left for the day the building inspector would have to reschedule, and the best they would tell us they could do was in three days. Did that hurt our company? Sure. But who it really hurt was the family who was waiting for their new home to be completed. The delay incurred would cost them another month of rent or temporary housing. Whatever the reason why the building inspector wanted to be an asshole, it only hurts the little guy and not the big developer. This hurtful delay was an inconvenience to the new homeowners that would cost money and aggravation.

When I was young and in school, there were always great teachers who wanted to torture you. Here you are, the first day of class after twelve long, gorgeous weeks of summer fun, and the teacher informs you that the first test will be on Friday. (For some reason, the first day of school always started on a Wednesday.) Here are two books to read over the next two days to prepare to take the test. Can you imagine having to study two two-hundred-page books and be prepared for a test

How to Recognize an Asshole

on Friday, two days later? Why, you ask, what is the reason? Will this really make me more prepared in life for a job or to be a better friend or parent? This teacher wanted to lay the groundwork for the rest of the year—who was the boss and what they expected out of this class. There are better ways to skin a cat than to be a straight- up asshole.

The most famous asshole on television is Larry David from the hit show Curb Your Enthusiasm. Having met him in person, I can say that he is simply perfect in this role. No matter where he goes in life, he plays the perfect role of an asshole and social assassin. He says whatever is on his mind with no qualms about the effect it has on people. Let us say that you are wearing a plaid shirt with striped pants. Anyone can see that this does not match, but who is going to come up and say something? Larry David, that's who. He would blurt, "Um, do you have a mirror in your house? I only say that because you must be blind if you do not know that stripes and plaids do not go together." Larry has no idea that he might hurt someone's feelings; in his world, he thinks he is helping the poor schmuck by telling them this outfit makes them look like a moron. The bottom line is that Larry is an asshole. There is no reason for Larry to offer an opinion and hurt this person's feelings. He should let the person do whatever they want as an expression of personal taste.

I have a real-life Larry David story. My brother-in-law (the best guy in the world) had a Larry David birthday party for his sixtieth birthday. My sister had a cake made with Larry David's picture photographed on top. It was amazing! (I took a picture of it with my phone.) The next weekend, my son and I are at a golf club near my home in Florida. There are many famous people here all the time, so there is high security with gates and security people everywhere. My son and I are in a small lunchroom, and there is only one other person sitting alone at a table—Larry David. Normally, I would not go up to someone, but we are in such an exclusive spot, and it is only the three of us sitting about nine feet apart in the same room, so I took the liberty of going over to him to show him a picture of my brother-in-law's birthday cake. I thought it was funny. He looks up at me and says, "Who do you think you are, bothering me during my lunch? Leave me alone." Embarrassed, I put my tail between my legs and sat back down at my table nine feet away.

Four hours later, my son (the club champion) and I were done golfing and went into the lunchroom for a beer. There are a few people in there, including Larry David and his golf group. I was not going anywhere near this guy. Out of the corner of my eye, I see him start to walk up to me. Now towering over me, he asks, "Can I talk to you privately?" Standing, I thought to myself, "What does this asshole want from me now? I already said I was sorry." Larry then proceeds to apologize to me for his behavior and gives me an autographed napkin to give my brother-in-law. I guess sometimes assholes realize they went too far and feel bad about it.

So, what can you learn from this chapter about dealing with assholes? First, we are all going to encounter assholes, whether in the workplace or in our personal lives. Second, we need to realize that the person is an asshole and then avoid them and the situation as quickly as possible. If we try to resolve the situation, like the restaurant manager did at the steak house, we might get a happy result, but we might not. Instead, try and make the asshole happy and then quickly move on. If you're a student and the teacher is an asshole, there is little that can be done; it is the start of a school year, and you are stuck with the situation. However, you now know what a future with this person looks like and how you must prepare in order to succeed. The building inspector is what it is, and there is nothing you can do but to keep trying and hopefully the guy will come around. My experience is to keep taking the punches and be nice and finally you will win because the building inspector will learn that he cannot get under your skin, and he will realize that you will cooperate under all the circumstances. Sure, you want to rage, but they will most certainly get you in a bigger hole. There is an expression "sit on your hand." The next day, deal with it when the rage has simmered down and you are more rational.

And when you meet the Larry David characters of the world (and there are a lot, but if I busted out every story there would be no one to read my book), try and manage the expectation. In my case, I was wrong to approach him. He was nice and very gracious at the end, but the first encounter was pure Larry David. I thought his character was just one on TV, but the reality is that he plays the part so well because he lives it.

CHAPTER 23
The Gift of Color

What's your favorite color? I ask this because everyone has a favorite color, whether it's the color of the clothes you wear or the color that you use to decorate your home. Wearing your favorite color, for instance, can not only make you look good—it can make you feel good too. Decorating a wonderful room in a spectacular color can motivate you and everyone who enters it. Color is one of the most exciting yet one of the most underutilized tools in life. The truth is that people use color a lot, but they do not think about it too much.

Let's say you're a businessperson. If you work in a corporate environment, most of the people you see there are wearing blue suits; it is almost like a uniform. Every morning, they wake up, put on their blue suit, wear a matching shirt (usually white or light blue), and add a tie. Now they are ready to take on the world.

Occasionally, you run into that one person who wears something flashy, say a red shirt or a bold tie. They do that for a reason—so people will notice them! That is what color does. Color is a statement; it forces others to notice you. This is an enormously powerful tool, both for your personal identity and for your business. Think of all the incredible ways we use color to promote ourselves and our businesses. Your marketing materials will stand out when printed with eye-catching colors, such as red or yellow. If you own a restaurant or

The Gift of Color

a shop, the awning outside can stand out to passersby if it's in a strong color. Any packaging you use to ship a product can have an enormous impact depending on its color.

Many businesses define themselves (and their logos) by using a specific color. Every time you see an orange Hermès shopping bag or the robin's-egg blue of a Tiffany & Co. ring box, you will immediately recognize it due to its very distinct trademark color. These companies have used color to create a niche; now that specific color of bag or box is a calling card for anyone walking down the street to see. Their product trademark is noticeably clear in the color of the bag. When you see it, it signifies an incredibly special and important purchase, as well as the importance of the person carrying the bag.

What does color say about a person in other instances? For example, what does the color of a car say about the person who drives it? If you see someone driving a red car, you might think of them as flashy. If someone has a white or a black car, you might consider them to be understated or distinguished. Someone drives by in a bright blue or purple car and you think, "Boy, are they trying to get some attention." This is how the color of a car represents the person who drives it, what they are all about, and what they want to portray.

Color is all around us, but people take it for granted. Many marketing companies start out with a plan to use color, but as the weeks of defining a product go by, suddenly color drops to the bottom of their list of priorities. Never ignore color. Color defines who you are and what you represent (or sell). It is the sizzle that is just as important as the steak. Think about it. When you walk down a store aisle and a package stands out from the shelves, it's because of its color. After noticing the package, you might not buy it, but since it stood out from the other products you did give it a chance. It's that moment of grabbing your attention and getting you to look that is a win-win.

In writing this book, I need to decide what the cover should look like. And, boy, is color important in this decision. For an established writer like James Patterson, it might not be important, but for a new writer like myself, I want to give my book the best shot. So, the cover and color are especially important. I spend a lot of time in bookstores looking at the covers of other books, trying to determine what will be in keeping this motivational book. I hope I learn a lesson from this chapter.

It is not so strange that everyone has a favorite color. For many, the choice of a favorite color is personal; others might pick a color because it complements their complexation, their hair, or their personality. Perhaps a certain color speaks to your background or heritage—you love the color green because you're Irish. Color is more than a word; it has real meaning with real emotions connected to it. People will wear black at a funeral...or at a very fancy evening event. Same color, different emotions. Yet for both types of events, black is necessary color.

Color is also used to define actions: red means stop, yellow advises caution, and green means go. Think of it as an unwritten language; everyone understands what those colors mean and how they should react.

Color is used in decorating of your home or apartment. The new trend at the writing of this book is white. Kitchens are all going white, houses are going all white contemporary and interiors are all white. Even though white is so plain it is dramatic.

Color is enormously powerful. It sends a message about you, your product, or any object. Use it as a hidden or secret language, one that everyone understands no matter which language you speak. Color is universal and transcends all barriers.

CHAPTER 24
Power: How Do You Know Who Has It?

This chapter is about power and the many ways we define it. The obvious exhibition of power is that of a political leader; and the most powerful political leader is the president of the United States. Since I live in Florida, my kids and I have had the pleasure of a front-row seat during the presidency of Donald Trump.

When I moved to Florida full time in 2004, I joined the Trump Palm Beach golf club at the Mar-a-Lago resort. The club was ground-zero for the giants of industry, including bankers, athletes, celebrities, and anyone else famous. At the time, no one cared that it was owned by Donald Trump; it just was a special place in Palm Beach with one of the best golf courses in the state.

When Donald Trump became the president of the United States, I witnessed first-hand the power of the office of the president and the most powerful man on planet earth!

For purpose of this story, let me lay out what Trump Palm Beach looks like. As you get off I-95 in Palm Beach, next to the Palm Beach International airport, you drive down a road call Summit Boulevard. About halfway down the road, you reach a gated entrance with a security hut, guards, and red cones. Once you clear the gate (if you are lucky), you cruise up a winding driveway to the covered entrance at the front of the clubhouse. Pre-presidency, this circular driveway was lined with forty or fifty exotic cars—from Lamborghinis to Rolls Royces and everything in between.

Once Donald Trump became president, everything changed. The member's cars were now parked on a nearby lot located on the club grounds. The circular driveway that used to hold the member's cars was now filled with a dozen Black SUVs. Armed men in full tactical military gear held machine guns, surface-to-air missiles, and anything else used to fight an attack. A few feet away sat an ambulance, a mobile surgery center with a full-time surgeon, a truck that had a shower to wash the president off (in case he is sprayed with poison), and a host of other cars in the caravan. Even if the president was out on the golf course, these cars kept their engines running, surrounded by military personnel clutching their weapons. This was a sight to see. Remember, this scene is not in a public setting; it's behind the gates of an exclusive club. I cannot even imagine what the president of the United States in a public setting would look like.

In addition to this, there are dozens of support staff for the president because wherever he goes so goes the office of the president of the United States. There are photographers to help create a presidential library and legacy. There is a military support staff to secure the communications required to be in touch with the presidents and key cabinet members at a moment's notice. There is even the somewhat frightening aspect of the military man who walks with in a few feet of the president and who carries a black briefcase called the "nuclear football" with the codes to launch a nuclear attack anywhere in the world. Finally, there are the personal assistants, the chief of staff, the food tasters, a personal chef, and a cast of characters whose job functions remain mysterious, other than that they were standing around with computers, pads, and pens.

When you entered the clubhouse, there were Secret Service agents everywhere. They would examine you with hand-held detection wands to ensure that you did not have any weapons on you. Within a foot of the front door, the Secret Service had commandeered one of the dining rooms and turned it into a command center with people and computers everywhere. It was very impressive. (I have never been in this room, but you can look in there while walking by as the door opens or when someone walks out.) Inside the small, forty-seat lunchroom, the president sits at a big round table, usually with four or five famous people holding court—everyone from professional golfers to senators or congresspeople, cabinet members, or foreign leaders. (I once saw Abe Shinzo, the former president of Japan, sitting within fifteen feet of me.) There are Secret Service agents everywhere. It's an insane scene to find yourself within fifteen or twenty feet of the most powerful man in the country and whatever powerful person he is with for that day. I have taken many guests there over the years. Most of them don't like or even hate Trump, but they are in complete awe of the power of the presidency and what it entails to protect and support of the most powerful man in the country.

As the president makes his way outside, the show continues. At least one hundred Secret Service agents follow him everywhere inside this exclusive private club. I can only imagine if a president is going to go out in public instead of the enclave of a super exclusive club, there must be protection that is multiple times of what we see today. The president walks over to the practice tee and golf green to warm up. There is chaos everywhere: Secret Service agents, club members that want to say hello, members and their guests who want a picture. Whether you love or hate Trump, he was always very gracious and able to take a photo, give a warm handshake, say hello, or embrace a young kid. What an unbelievable thrill to get your photo taken with the most powerful man in the world, especially if you are a young man or lady.

Now, it is off to golf. There are least forty golf carts filled with armed Secret Service agents encircling the president while he plays golf. The Secret Service agents are dressed in full military gear with helmets, bulletproof vests, machine guns, and rocket launchers to take down drones. They must be prepared for any type of attack at any moment. This is the extreme power of the office of the president in full force. Anyone who gets this job receives all of this protection plus the staff, Air Force One, Marine One, the White House, Camp David, and everything else that goes with the job.

While all this chaos is going on outside, inside the building there is a temporary command center with about twenty-five people. This command center moves with the president; it goes wherever he goes and with so much electronic equipment that it would blow your mind. Virtually every sort of communication vehicle is present, so if the president needs to contact his generals or a foreign leader or basically anyone at moment's notice, they are prepared to make this happen in seconds.

The point of this chapter is not about Donald Trump but about the power of the presidency. It is truly inspiring to see how a president is protected and treated. It's one thing to see this presidential protection portrayed on a TV show or in a movie, but to be fifteen feet away and able to observe it in person is mind blowing. I was required to share personal information in order to be approved to enter the building while the president was there. At the winter dinner dances, members had to pull into the parking lot, then drive into a tent where Secret Service agents with dogs would check under the hood of your car, inside the trunk, and underneath the chassis with a mirror.

Power finds its face in other avenues of life besides the presidency and exists in many forms, from a restaurant host who controls when you're seated and where, to a police officer or a bouncer at a bar, to the CEO of a Fortune 500 company. Power rests in the type of job they have and what they can control. It rests in what and where your life goes at that moment.

Imagine you are a billionaire CEO of some Fortune 500 company. You show up at some restaurant in New York without a reservation, and there is a one-hour wait for a seat. Usually, it does not matter who or what you are when you are faced with the prospect of standing in line or getting a drink until a table is available. The manager or host of this restaurant has power over your life and your time. When you're at work, you are a big deal; your schedule is packed by the minute with everyone wanting to talk to you. Yet, here at this very moment, you are subject to wasting one hour while waiting for your table (unless you can tip your way in quicker). You quickly understand this is a much different type of power, but it is still power.

Over the last twenty years, we had a house in the Hamptons for the summer. My kids were in college and wanted to go to the hottest nightclubs on the weekend. The hottest ones were the Stephen Talkhouse and Surf Lodge. Guess what? At the front door, there was a big bouncer. He was the chief guy who would decide if you were going to gain entrance to the hottest nightclub in the Hamptons. Now, this guy was not CEO smart or celebrity famous, but in his job, he had total control over my kids and their friends' lives for the evening. It was his decision to either let my kid in the door or send her away crying all the way back to our house. This a different type of power, but it is still power.

Everyone knows what power looks like. It could look like a police officer or a judge, a building inspection officer, or the person at the DMV who decides how to deal with an infraction. The people in those positions get to decide.

The question you might ask is how the subject of power is part of this book. The answer is quite simple. Power is a force. You must understand and recognize how it works and how to deal with it. Do not fight the system and assume it will work out. The people who have power can make your life miserable. If you recognize where the power dynamics are, you will always be successful. Yelling at a police officer and threatening to take down his badge number and trying to get him fired will get you nowhere. Instead, try to be reasonable and accommodating instead of argumentative. The same goes with a restaurant host or a manager or anyone who has control of your time. Breathe deep, take a moment, and try to figure out who has the power in any given situation. Then use that knowledge to your advantage to obtain your goals.

CHAPTER 25
Movies Are Fun, Exciting, and Relaxing

Watching a movie offers a much-needed relief from stress and provides enjoyment at the same time. A great movie allows you to take a two-hour (or more) time-out in life. I have seen many excellent movies that are funny, sad, inspirational, or motivational. In authoring this book about motivation, I think back on all of the movies that had a profound impact on the how I live my life every day. Whenever I feel blue, taking the time out of the day to watch a movie (or even a TV series) gives me get strength and inspiration to fight another day. One of the greatest movies franchises is the series of *Rocky* films. I have personally seen every *Rocky* and *Creed* movie many times over, and each time I discover something new—something that I had never caught before in any of the films.

One day, I was on the practice tee at my Florida golf course when who comes walking up with his golf bag over his shoulder? None other than Sylvester Stallone, the newest member of our golf club (he had just moved to Florida from California). I have seen many famous people in my life, including in the Hamptons in the summer and elsewhere in Florida, and most of them look like any other person walking down the street. But Sylvester Stallone looks like a bona fide movie star. He is built like a brick shithouse, bulging with muscles from head to toe, and wearing blue-pleated pants, a tight short-sleeve

Movies Are Fun, Exciting, and Relaxing

Kiton shirt, and the most gorgeous alligator golf shoes I had ever seen. To top it off, he wore a great French cap that matched his entire outfit.

Normally, I am not intimidated by anyone, but being alone with "Rocky" on a golf practice tee blew me away. In a place like this fancy golf club in Palm Beach, which I have been going to for seventeen years, people do not want to be bothered. But this was one my true idols, and one of the greatest (and highest-grossing) action heroes was now standing fifteen feet away from me. I felt like a kid on a first date with no idea what to do. So, I did nothing other than practice my shots next to Sly on the range.

Next thing I know, one of the caddies that I am friendly with comes down to the range to caddie nine holes for Mr. Stallone. As the caddie approaches the range, he bellows out my name, "Good afternoon, Mr. C!" The caddie then says hi to Sly (I guess he regularly caddies for him) and proceeds to introduce us. We exchange a quick hello, where I try to impress Sly right from the jump: I am from Philadelphia (the Rocky movies are based in Philadelphia); I am a graduate of the University of Miami (Sly also went there); and my birthday is in July, just one day away from Sly's birthday. Sly was very gracious, but he obviously couldn't care less; he just wanted to play golf. Often, if a club member is golfing alone, they will ask another member to join them on their round of golf. In this instance, Sly's caddie asked me if I wanted to join them to play the front nine holes of golf, and I very excitedly said yes. Suddenly, we were off to the first tee!

We rode in two separate golf cars, so we did not have much interaction on the nine holes other than on the putting greens where we took our respective turns. We joked and laughed a little, and the nine holes were over in a flash. Sly could not have been nicer and, as we said our goodbyes, and said, "Let's do it again soon." Whether or not he meant it, it was a genuinely nice thing to say, and I shared my schedule (I work every day, played the course during the week at about 4 p.m.). This was during the fall of 2021, amid the COVID-19 pandemic. The Florida governor, Ron DeSantis, kept the state relatively open throughout the pandemic and, obviously, one of the more popular things to do outside was to play golf.

Over the next several months, I looked for Sly Stallone every time I went to the club, but he was filming a new TV series and was not on the range. I started to think about ideas for a Rocky sequel. There were so many things happening in the world that could apply to a new script: The violence and riots in cities at the forefront of the Black Lives Matter movement; the drama and death as a result of the COVID-19 pandemic; people losing their jobs left and right because all work was suspended unless you worked remotely; flare-ups with the police, prison reform, and everything in the wake of the murder of George Floyd. All of these events created a huge divide in our country.

As the pandemic raged on, there was extraordinarily little to do but take walks, play some golf, and watch movies. I watched all of the new movies and many of the old ones. I started re-watching films series such at The Godfather, Rambo, and of course all of the Rocky movies. I was most intrigued by the Rocky movies and sequels. There were so many ideas roaring through my head, blending many of the old Rocky characters with new ones, and interweaving all of the problems of the world with in the four corners of my script creating drama and excitement in the story lines.

One day I had a bright idea. I had now met Sylvester Stallone in person. I had also seen all of the Creed and Rocky movies many times over. I should write a new Rocky sequel in real time. I started slowly, having never written anything more substantial than long, intense business letters. Things started to move faster as ideas percolated in my head. Finally, one day I started writing at a rapid pace determined to finish my script/outline that same day. That day, I sat at the computer for ten hours until I finished my story.

Once the outline for the sequel was done, I prepared to give it to Sly. If he liked my concept, it could be written into an actual script. I contacted Sly, and he informed me he was just an employee of the Rocky franchise, although a highly compensated one. I would have to forward my ideas on to the people who held the rights to the Rocky franchise. They would review and determine the next steps if interested. This is where we are at the writing of this book.

CHAPTER 26
The Podcast!

During the summer, a friend of thirty years who also lives in Florida called me and asked me if I wanted to do a podcast with him. I said, "What the hell is a podcast?" I guess out of Covid with everyone sitting around and doing nothing the concept of the podcast was expanded. With production shut down on so many TV shows and movies, there was a new lane for content as people were bored and needed something to do and watch. This friend was someone who I spoke to several times a week, and we just talked and talked on the phone like two teenage girls. The subject matter was broad. It was girls, it was guys, it was current events, and it was sports. My friend, who we affectionately call "Govy" is in the watch business, or I should say is the largest Patek Phillipe and Rolex watch dealer in the world with stores all around the world and of course on the internet. Out of his relationship in the watch business, Govy sells these very expensive and premium watches to the celebrities and athletes of the world. I always enjoyed the stories and fantasies of these celebrities and their spending habits. Govy had all the stories.

Govy, recently married for his final time, received as a wedding gift from his wife a gift certificate for a free podcast session in a podcast studio here in South Florida. The phone call was simply to see if I would be his cohost on the free show for fun. Obviously, talking twice a week, we both were comfortable with each other and had a great banter back and forth that was informative and very funny.

A date was set for our show. We approached this podcast with a great degree of seriousness and did an extensive outline of the material we wanted to cover. We did the show and had so much fun that we sent it around to all of our friends and family to review and give us their constructive comments. The reviews came back strong, so we decided to buy a package of eight studio sessions to do some more podcasts.

As I write this book, we have forty-three episodes that can be found on YouTube, Instagram, Tik Tok, Apple, Spotify, and Facebook. It is hard to believe, but we now have over 300,000 listeners and are podcast superstars... (Just joking, but getting there.)

Our show is called The CuttyandGovy Show, and we tape it once a week and our team posts it on the various social media outlets within twenty-four hours. As we started doing more and more shows, it became less and less of a project and more of a spontaneous adventure of two friends sitting in front of the camera with microphones just laughing and having fun. In this book, there is a picture of our caricature logo that is the start and finish of every show. We have some music that starts our show and ends our show. Very cool stuff.

Some of our best shows were shows that we did not predict the outcome but just came off great. About half of our shows had guest appearances, and I can honestly say we have yet to have a bad guest.

Our first guest was a woman psychologist who not only was very smart but was easy on the camera, as they say. She covered the entire issue of work from home after Covid and the entire controversy surrounding companies and employees on different sides of the issue. During Covid, people got used to working efficiently remotely, as well as enjoying the freedom of staying at home and enjoying life a little more than in a sterile work environment. Obviously, there is more time with their spouse or significant other, more time with their children or parents, and of course more time with their pets. When Covid had subsided and companies wanted employees to come back to work full time, the PTSD of that world came roaring out with people not wanting to separate from their new life. Our guest, who treats people with this particular PTSD had incredible stories of the successes and failures and the drama that people are going through trying to readjust to the normal work environment that has existed forever.

This was a terrific show with many great observations and tips on the adjustment. The bottom line is that people really had a decision to make if their company insisted on their return to the office. Suck it up and return to the office or find a new job. Crazy, but that has become the new reality if a hybrid work environment was not acceptable to the company.

Our next guest was a guy I met at my golf course who did not look the part for sure. My golf course is located in Palm Beach, and you might say that it would be considered one of the finest golf courses in the state of Florida. I only say that to set the stage in explaining our next guest. This gentleman is one of the most amazing stories about perseverance that I have met or experienced in my life. Physically, Matt is covered head to toe in tattoos, is about 6'2, and is built and looks like a Ralph Lauren model with tattoos. As I got to know Matt, I learned about his story, which he tells in great detail on our podcast. Matt in his younger years was a heroin and crack addict, alcoholic, cocaine addict, and was homeless. His story is about his journey through twenty plus rehabs trying to kick his addiction until he finally met someone who was able to get through to him and change his life. From this point forward, Matt became a prolific motivational speaker and drug counselor, helping others kick their addictions one day at a time. The story on reclaiming his life one day at a time to become clean, sober, and a multimillionaire was inspiring and compelling. It is a Rocky story about real life that takes a bad left turn and somehow turns right to go down the middle. Matt goes on to own rehabs and speaks to people who he needs to help. In some ways, his recovery is tied to his speaking and teaching every day. By being present and involved he is always conscience of the ugly side of his disease and the destructive path that it contains. Being around Matt is a true inspiration, teaching anyone who does not carry these burdens how much easier it is to scrape yourself off and fight every day to survive and succeed.

Prior to myself and my cohost going sober, we spent a ton of time in restaurants and bars. Both of us miss those days, but we are much better without the booze than with it. Going out every night, you become friends with all the bartenders in town. One such bartender, Mitch, came on our show to explain life in Palm Beach on the opposite side of the bar! Wow, this was a fun show and hilarious to say the least. Mitch, one of the more popular bartenders in town and has made more than $200,000 per year since the age of twenty-two working in the fancy, swinging popular restaurants in town. Over the years he has built up a loyal following of customers that request his section if he is on the floor or get seats at his bar the nights that he is working the bar.

His stories about the hookers, the old guys, the divorcees, the one-liners used, the bad toupees, and the giants of industry were compelling. The inner workings of being on that side of the bar is fascinating. Not only is there a code of silence of people's names and associations, but there is the discretion that must always take place when one side of a couple is cheating on the other side. Evidently, this is a common occurrence, and the dancing someone in the industry has to do to stay out of the crossfire is remarkable. Not only that, but Mitch, being also a very well built and good-looking guy, gets propositioned all the time by older women seeking company. I have to joke around with him, when trying to figure out how much money per year he could make being a matchmaker or studding himself out for evenings with the older women who have tons of money.

Throughout the show, we asked a million questions, but the one that got the most feedback from our 300,000 plus listeners was how much should the tip be for a bottle of wine. Let's say for example we are a table of four, and we order two bottles of wine for $150 per bottle, which today believe it or not is probably just an average bottle of wine in Palm Beach. Do you tip 10% or 20% or no percent of the cost of $300. Think about it, a $60 tip for pouring wine into a glass?

Well, Mitch has a much different view of tipping on wine. To serve wine is an art. The customer should be presented with the bottle properly. The customer should not only get good recommendations on choices with their specific meal but the opportunity to understand each type of wine and in some instances if it is available by the glass to try a sample. Finally, there is an art to pouring the wine and making sure your customer never touches the bottle or has to ask for a refill of his glass. It must be automatic. Based on the above facts, it appears a 20% tip or more is appropriate for a bottle of wine.

The best conversation is about the patrons who come in (no names mentioned). A patron could come in with his wife and have a nice dinner. A week later, the same patron can come in with a date and sit at the bar as if nothing is wrong. The is no "your regular, Mr. Jones?" or "how is the family Mr. Jones?" It is as if you do not know the guy. Then a week later the same patron may come back in with his wife because she is back in town, and again nothing can ever be said, like it was great to see you last week. I said to Mitch, "How do you keep it straight?" His response, "This is what I do for a living, and I understand the rules of the game. It pays to keep my mouth shut for two reasons. Reason number 1 is I keep my job. Reason number 2 is I usually get a big tip!"

Govy, many years ago had a gentleman selling watches for him right out of school. This young man worked for Govy and his brother for about two years then left and got a job working in the porn industry selling video tapes, getting a feel for a different industry. Obviously, the video business disappeared with the new technology, so Adam transitioned into the sex toy industry. Fast forward thirty years, he is the largest sex toy manufacturer and distributor in the United States. The fun part about this was that Govy got him on our show! What a blast. Adam did the show by video remote from office. I had never met Adam or spoken to him, but your mind wonders when you are imagining a show and what this porn business owner looks like and sounds like. Obviously you cannot help yourself thinking it is some sleazy guy in a trench coat. To my surprise, Adam had short hair, a nice, collared shirt and pants on and was professional, clean cut, and well spoken. For the next hour, he went on to regale us of all the stories about his products, the industry, the items that are hot and not, and the basic inner workings of his company. On the outside it sounds like a notorious business, but when you hear Adam explain his business in detail, he could be selling stuff animals or tires for cars. There are hot products, there is shipping and storage, there is inventory, just the same as any other business.

Obviously, we did get into detail what the new hottest items are. What the most popular colors are (red, of course) what the most profitable occasions are i.e. Valentine's Day, birthdays, Christmas, anniversaries, on and on.

As a bona fide business, the margins are insane! Adam buys his most popular item call the "Rose." This is an air-infused rose that cost him $12. He sells it for $59. Crazy money. The Rose is a battery-operated air-infused dildo that has taken his industry by storm.

The show was so fun, but more importantly was the lessons learned from Adam's story. Nothing he is doing is illegal. He has giant warehouses loaded with products in boxes, trucks, and drivers. He sells to 15,000 sex toy stores across the country. Apparently, in this business, people want instant gratification and prefer to go into a retail store and look around and buy what they like. Obviously, they have an online store, but that primarily is for people who have bought products in the past and want to buy it again. I can honestly say after spending one hour with Adam, I thoroughly enjoyed being a podcast superstar and being able to meet and interview such interesting people. A person can take an industry that you would think is disgusting and gross and run it professionally and make a fortune. This was an amazing experience that showed me firsthand that any legal business can be a real business if run professionally.

Over the one year and forty-three episodes that our podcast has existed, I have begged my four children to come on as guests. The first three graduated, Columbia, Brown, and University of Pennsylvania. The fourth who is arguably the smartest with just receiving a perfect score on his SAT is bound for Princeton or another IVY league institution. The only one who accepted my invitation was my son who graduated from the University of Pennsylvania as an economics major and works on Wall Street. What I learned most from his college experience was not the incredible education he received but that it was the bond and closeness he found and relishes with his frat boys. All these kids are brilliant and are making a fortune for twenty-four-year-olds, but it is the human bonds that make their experience so special. In their relationship with their frat mates, they navigated the social, school studies, and now business experiences of life, having each other to count on and learn from with both giving advice and getting advice from each other. They all went through the breakups with girls, all nighters for exams, and of course all the drinking and partying that goes on living together at a frat house.

Cutty Jr and Govy have known each other for years, as we all raised our kids in the same neighborhood, so it was an easy fit having Cutty Jr on the show. Admittedly, although Govy and I think we are hip and in tune with the world, it is a much different place and time then when we grew up. No one had cell phones, computers, dating sites, rap music etc. The only thing we had in common was booze and sports. It was such an interesting show discussing the problems on campuses such as antisemitism, racial problem, transgender issues, stress of school, social situations, and of course finding a job and going out into the world. What was such a fun subject obviously is sports. College ball for both men and women is huge and exciting. Of course, we had to talk about professional sports and the crazy money that is now being paid to today's ballplayers. These kids really have a great grasp of the stats and the fun being a fan and spectator.

The show ended with Cutty Jr testing Govy on a trivia question that was tough as they come. Govy, who has a photographic memory, stepped up to the plate and answered seven out of seven. The question was, which seven colleges produced not only a president but a Super Bowl winning quarterback? Watch the Cutty and Govy podcast to see how Govy thought his way to victory!

CHAPTER 27

From Beginning to the Not-So-Nice End

My dad is ninety-two years old, and my mom is ninety years old. Every Saturday, I try to have lunch with them. Let me set the scene so you understand where my parents are in life.

About fifteen years ago, I was building some houses in a country club community down here in Florida. The economy was starting to go into a recession, and I could not sell the last two houses. My parents lived down the street in a more modest community where the homes were selling for about $300,000.

One day I was having a discussion with my father, and I said, "Look, I cannot sell this great house on a great lakefront lot. Why don't you sell your house and move into the new home? Then when the market turns around, we can start to think about selling this house for a big profit." At the time, my dad was seventy-seven. I figured that in ten years he would be in some sort of assistant living facility, so why not enjoy the next ten years in this wonderful home?

Things did not work out that way. First, my mother had a stroke; she was in rehab for about six months. My dad was all alone at the time, and his home was a safe place for him. My mother came home in a wheelchair. They had to have round-the-clock aides take care of her because she could not walk, dress herself, make food, etc. Then

From Beginning to the Not-So-Nice End

my dad had a series of falls over the next few years. He started to "lose his brains," as they say in the health care world. He had Alzheimer's. He continued to fall for the next few years, and the Alzheimer's, which I had thought would progress slowly, happened rather quickly.

One day, he was walking out of a doctor's office, and he could not find his car in the parking lot. He went back into the doctor's office and asked for help. They called me, and I came over and found his car and drove him home. Without our permission, the doctor wrote a letter to the state telling them to revoke his driver's license because he was losing his brains quickly. The state sent a letter that took away his driver's license and, I guess, his independence too, as he saw it. Losing your license and the right to drive—to be independent—is a huge loss for someone who is older. Now, for the rest of your life, you must depend on other people to drive you around, rather than walking outside and jumping into your car to drive away.

The next thing I know, my father has another bad fall and is in the hospital for a month and then in a rehab for a month. At this point, he can't walk and didn't know what was going on. The exceptionally fine rehab facility determined that there was nothing more they could do for my father. A rehab facility is a temporary place meant to get you in a position to either move back into your own home or into a nursing home. In my father's situation, we brought him back to his home, but he now required full-time care.

So here we are. He is at home with an aide who comes in the morning for twelve hours and an aide who comes at night for twelve hours. My mother has the same schedule with aides in the morning and at night. Other than going to the doctors, which they are driven to by their aides, their only activity of the day is to go to lunch at the clubhouse and then go home and nap before waking for dinner. Then they go to bed for the night.

I try and go to the clubhouse every Saturday and join them for lunch. The scene looks like this: At the table are my parents, who are both in wheelchairs and diapers, the two aides, and me. The aides enjoy themselves thoroughly at this luxurious country club buffet. My parents barely eat, and when they do take a bite of something, they are usually being fed by the aide. They can drink soda through a straw and eat a cookie for dessert, but using a knife and fork is out of the question. I assume that they also both have Parkinson's, as my mother especially shakes. My father sits at the lunch table in a diaper and a wheelchair, unable to eat by himself, unable to talk because of Parkinson's, unable to hear, unable to recognize his best friend, me, or anyone else. The only person that he does seem to know is my mother.

This takes me to my point. My sister's daughter just had a baby, an unbelievably cute kid. My kids are older now, and I forgot about all the nuances of raising a child, all the equipment and stuff like formula and diapers and strollers and car seats that are required to have a child. I think of the two of them together, and it suddenly dawns on me. You start life just like this little baby in diapers: unable to understand anything, unable to eat on your own, unable to dress yourself, take a bath or shower, or take care of yourself in general. Then you go through life and have children or a career, maybe you're even the president of the United States. Then, after you live this long life, at the end you are a baby again. You wear a diaper, you cannot walk, you cannot eat by yourself, you cannot really communicate. As an old man, you replicate who you were when you were a baby. Life has come full circle. You start out in diapers, and you end in diapers. Life is the middle of an adventure and it is what you make of it.

I sit there and look at my dad and my sister's daughter's son. They are in the same exact place, except they are ninety-two years apart. My dad had a wonderful life, a respectable job, a wife and three children, and he cannot remember any of it. He needs people to support him and to take care of his every need; he exists as if he is a baby.

I guess the moral of this chapter is to have the best life—in the middle of your life—that you can. If you are lucky, you will have fun and live a long life. If you are unlucky, you will die too young or live too long without quality of life. I have had a front row seat to living too long with no quality of life. It is horrible and is a huge burden on the family. Our family is lucky, and we have resources, but it is still stressful.

There is an expression used stated below

If you die in your thirties, it is very tragic.

If you die in your forties, it is sad and tragic.

If you die in your fifties, it is such a shame.

If you die in your sixties, it is too soon.

If you die in your seventies, boy, you had a good run.

If you die in your eighties, it is a life well lived.

If you die in your nineties, boy, was that a hell of a ride!

Make the best of your life!

CHAPTER 28

Your Amazing Body and Mind

Whoever you believe created us, there is one thing for sure. The final product, a human being, is beyond exceptional. Our creator gave us the ability to heal in both body and mind.

Let us start with a wound as simple as a cut on a finger. The body has a remarkable ability to regenerate, to heal the wound and make it disappear within days or at the most weeks. How does this happen? Very recently, I was in the kitchen slicing peppers with a very sharp knife. I did not have a good grip on the pepper I was slicing (also, drinking a martini) and the knife slipped and caught my finger. It sliced very deeply into my finger. At this point, I said to myself, "I need a few stitches to close this wound." Having had a few drinks, I was less concerned about my sliced finger than I should have been. At age 65, I take a baby aspirin every day, as most older people do for their heart health. A side effect of aspirin is that it makes you bleed more than usual. Here I am with blood gushing out of my finger, using a paper towel as a tourniquet to try and slow the bleeding, as it is gushing out at a good pace.

I rummage through the kitchen drawers, looking for a bandage or anything I can use to stop the bleeding, and I come upon two amazing products that I wish I had as a kid. The first one is a glue for cuts. The

Your Amazing Body and Mind

second one is a liquid bandage that can be applied to difficult areas that are hard to fit a bandage.

Again, being drunk, I sloppily applied the glue to the slice, squeezed the cut together as hard as I could, and held it there for several minutes. Amazingly, it stuck together! I sat down, had another drink, and continued to hold the wound closed for about a half hour. It held beautifully. Then I applied the liquid bandage to the sliced finger, and it was temporarily healed for the night. I figured that, in the morning when I sobered up, I would assess the situation and decide if I needed to go to the hospital. I knew it was a nice little slice but not deep enough that my finger was going to fall off. When I woke up the first thing in the morning, I checked my beautiful white sheets to see if they were soaked in blood. The answer was no. Then I looked at my finger and saw that it was glued together very nicely and was on its way to healing.

Two weeks later, the scabs fell off the sliced finger. If you did not stare at it, you would never know anything had happened to me. The wound healed perfectly. To be honest, I am no scientist or doctor, and I know nothing about the human body. The only thing I can tell you is that this badly sliced finger healed as if nothing had ever happened. I was both utterly amazed and confused. How does this process occur? And how is it possible that your finger can regenerate to its formal normal self? The human body has the amazing power to heal.

I have never had surgery, but many of my friends have had major surgery, such as open-heart surgery, or have broken limbs that were all able to be put back together. But over time, the body did the bulk of healing. Modern medicine put the pieces in place, and our bodies' healing powers did the rest.

Think about the components of the human body. The skin is the outer layer that keeps the rest of the body parts safe inside your body. If something pierces this outer layer of skin, the blood inside comes gushing out. Think about all your body organs: the kidneys, the liver, the heart. They all have their place and stay in one spot; they do not move around. For example, the kidney is held in place by connective tissue called the renal fascia. This is surrounded by a thick layer of adipose tissue. How was all of this created in a human body? Why does hair grow on a man's legs and back (and sometimes your butt), but when you're older, it does not grow where you really want it—on your head!

Think about a woman's reproductive organs. It is amazing that a woman can grow a human being inside of her womb for nine months. The concept is hard to wrap your head around if you think about it. Two things are amazing about sex: It is so much fun, and you can also create a human being from the experience.

However, our physical bodies were created, the same healing effects are there for our mind. It is unbelievable how emotions have the ability to heal over time. Obviously, nothing goes away completely as it might in a wound. You may end up with scars, and the same thing happens with your emotions. A longtime scar happens in your mind, but you still have the ability to heal.

Take for instance the death of a loved one. When it occurs, you cannot breathe; you think you will never get through the emotional upheaval of the loss. Over time, the emotions soften to the point that it can become a memory you cherish, but not one to grieve over every day. You start to get past the shock of the death and to remember the wonderful things about the person and how important they were in your life.

Another example is a romantic break up. Those are the worst. There is no pill you can take, there is nothing you can do but walk around in circles for days wondering why, how, or what happened. There is nothing to get rid of the churn in your belly or the feelings of emptiness. Talking with trusted friends or family passes the time and helps the process move on. That's the only thing that you can do—allow the process to move forward, and over time the emotional loss will heal. Years later, you will look back on that romantic experience in many ways, but the immediate pain or loss will be only a memory. As you move forward into new relationships, you bring the memory and the experience of past relationships, good or bad. You may have your "guard up" or not allow yourself to be "all in" due to the tremendous pain experienced in your last break up. Everyone deals with this emotion differently; adjust the best you can.

This chapter is on healing in both the body and mind. Healing takes time, but rest assured that it will happen. You will become a better person for an experience that requires healing, no matter how unpleasant it was in your life. Time has a way of moving on hour-by-hour, day by day, left foot by right foot. One thing you cannot stop is time. Time moves on, and so does the healing process. Embrace the fact that, over time, you will heal or resolve the issues that were so dramatic when they occurred.

CHAPTER 29

Therapy: A Personal Relationship with Yourself

Have you watched the actor Charlie Sheen in the TV show *Two and a Half Men*? In one of the many great episodes, Charlie goes to a shrink (a therapist), and she calls him out on all the crazy and horrible things that he does in his life. It is hysterical! I urge you to watch the episode. As in most instances, people finding their way to a shrink due to issues with their relationship or to dealing with life. In Charlie's case, it is always dealing with his mother, his various girlfriends, and his brother.

A shrink is an excellent person to have in your life. It offers the ability to see your problems in a different light and an opportunity to face them head-on with a trained person, rather than run away from them or ignore them. Not to make all the shrinks who are reading this book mad, but I find it more useful to talk to a shrink than a good friend or family member. You always want a good friend or family member to love you, to respect you, and more importantly to like you. A shrink is an independent third party; you do not have to care if they like you. You get to tell them your innermost secrets, expel all of your complaints and issues, and examine the facts of your life; they give you professional advice, and you give them money. It is a great business arrangement. The relationship allows you to go deep and find a way to get better or to get over your problems.

Therapy: A Personal Relationship with Yourself

Let us say you are at a shrink's office for depression and contemplate something as horrible as suicide. You would rarely tell a spouse or a friend about these thoughts for fear they would go into a panic, or you might feel embarrassed to admit your weaknesses. If you see a shrink, then you can share your innermost thoughts with them because you do not have to fear their reaction or rejection, or any of their feelings on the matter. It is an honest, bare-knuckles confession that seeks advice and help.

Over the years, I've gone to at least ten different shrinks for various reasons and at different points in my life. The shrinks have been an even split between men and women, ranging from a beauty queen to a heavier old man with a long beard whose picture should sit next to the word "shrink" in the dictionary. Some were great, some were good, and some were narcissistic. One incredibly famous shrink, who has since pasted away, was impossible to see, as he was constantly booked. Finally, after years of trying, I was able to get a regular time with him. He was wonderful and thoughtful and always appeared interested in what I had to say. At the same time, he might have been the most narcissistic person I had ever met in my life. It got to the point where it was incredibly disturbing.

Several times, I stopped our session and said, "Don, not to be disrespectful, but this is about me, not you. I really do not want to hear about you all session long. I want to talk about my problems." Don always gazed at me, not believing that I would call a famous person such as him out for something like this. But, being a professional, he always regrouped, like a golfer who had hit a bad shot. He came back to the session immediately and helped me through my issues.

The point is that if you are not satisfied with where you are going with your shrink, then speak out. Do not waste your time. I was paying for this person's time with good money. I was there to do the work on myself, not to hear about my shrinks' accomplishments all session. He was not my friend. If I am there to do the work and get better, then he needs to be there too. Why not realign the session by calling him out to get back on track? That is a huge takeaway in life. If you are seeking professional advice, get what you need. Do not be polite and just sit there. Get them back on track helping you.

Through college and the early part of my career, I had a problem with quaaludes. What is a quaalude, you may ask? A quaalude is a muscle relaxer that gives you an incredible tingling feeling and makes you feel like a million dollars. Thankfully, they do not make them anymore. (The upside is that sex on quaaludes is an insane experience like no other.) I have a couple of experiences with quaaludes that I would like to share.

Early in my career, I was in a business relationship with a wealthy single guy who was very eccentric. I was doing extremely well, and so was he. We owned a piece of ground together and were trying to get it approved to develop into a housing community. He liked to have our meetings at his house because that was where his office was. One day, I am at his house and see on the fireplace mantle an unsealed bottle of one hundred brand-new quaaludes Now, quaaludes were impossible to get since the government had stopped the company, Rorer Pharmaceutical, from making them anymore. I asked him to sell me the bottle. He said no. I told him I would pay him $10,000 cash! He still said no. I left the house more dejected about the non-purchase of the quaaludes than the business deal, which was in an exceedingly difficult stage of approvals.

Longs story short, business got bad for this guy. He was in such a complicated mess that he ended up killing himself. For some reason,

Therapy: A Personal Relationship with Yourself

the Shiva (the Jewish practice of going to someone's house for several days after they die) was at his home, even though he didn't have a wife or children, just a sister. His parents had died years ago. I was sitting on the sofa in the family room, and there in front of me was the unsealed bottle of quaaludes still sitting on the mantle, the same bottle that I tried to buy from him about a year prior.

I thought to myself, "This house is going to get sold, and everything will be thrown out. No one knows what these quaaludes are. I am going to stick them in my heavy winter coat when I leave and will be one happy guy." I thought about it all night! By the end of the night, I just couldn't do it. I left the house without the bottle and thought about it all the way home. To this day, I feel that I made the right choice. I knew it was the right thing to do out of respect for my dead friend, who did not want me to have the bottle even when I said I would pay $10,000 for it.

My addiction to quaaludes raged on, and I went to a shrink for help. You could still buy them in the underground economy, but they were different from those sold in a sealed bottle. I was thirty years old, a small builder at the time, and my career was going well. I only did quaaludes at night and had it under control; I could function during the day, but at night all bets were off. I knew I had a problem, but with my busy career I did not have the time to enter into a rehab facility for thirty or sixty days. I was a new company with only a handful of employees; checking into a rehab for sixty days was a non-starter.

One Saturday night, I am at a nightclub called Elan in center city Philadelphia. It was a hot spot with tons of beautiful people. My shrink had been urging me to get into a drug program, not put myself in a situation like this nightclub scene. I realized that the shrink was right and that my quaalude problem was starting to slow down my career. I started making a ton of money in my career, and things started switching around in my mind. The new money was a bigger high than the quaaludes, but they were happening at various times of the day. The career during the day, the quaaludes at night. Then I had an epiphany. I am at this hot nightclub and am high as a kite on quaaludes. The drugs are starting to wear off, and I want to do another half a pill. I go into the men's room and enter a toilet stall. I grab my last quaalude and break it in half. As I do that, the quaalude slips out of my hand and falls into the toilet. I look at this quaalude sitting at the bottom of a disgusting toilet in a public bathroom and quickly plunge my hand into the toilet to save my last quaalude. In that very moment, I realized I was almost hopeless for doing something so disgusting. Here I had a great career, was making tons of money, was only thirty years old, and I am plunging my hand into a toilet to save a quaalude.

Many of us know that we have problems but are embarrassed to make the hard choice to fix them. When you are faced with this dilemma, you need to search for the answers that will get out of your situation and forward into a better life. There are a million self-help books, there are some great churches, and there are rehabs and shrinks. The goal is to admit you need help and fix yourself. In my case, I had two things going for me. I had an amazing career at a notably early age, where I started making millions of dollars per year and was able to do almost anything I wanted, from buying dinners, buying cars, taking vacations (which I rarely did because I was working all the time), or buying drugs...ugh.

The second thing I had going for me was that I knew right from wrong because I had spent so much time talking to shrinks. When I woke up the next day and remembered that I had plunged my hand into a public toilet, used by tons of people at this crowded club, just to get a quaalude so I could stay high, it was the end. If I needed to do something so disgusting just to stay high, then I was in a dangerous spot. From that night on, whenever I had an opportunity to take a quaalude I always thought of my arm swishing into a disgusting toilet, not even taking the time to roll up my sleeve to get a quaalude so I could stay high. I never did quaaludes again.

It was a horrible séance moment, but it did the trick. I was lucky. It could have been a lot worse, like a car accident or hurting someone you loved or overdosing and dying. I was blessed that a hand in a dirty toilet was enough for me to go straight. The craziest things in life have a way of turning out great. I could have shrugged this episode off, as I did so many times before. But I didn't. When something hits you in the face so hard, you need to see it and act. I was not a loser, but plunging my hand into a public toilet to just stay high would make me one. It is a shame that it came to something like this, but it scared me straight.

People may ask why I put this in a book and told people what happened. I think it will help someone else realize they are in trouble. Admission is a great compromise of facts and reality. My admission is now out there, and it puts me in a position where it would be hard to do something like that ever again. Look in the mirror and be honest with yourself. Mirrors do not lie.

CHAPTER 30
Dear Warren Buffett

I had always wanted to move back to Florida, which is where I had gone to college. I just loved the feel of the South and the people who lived there. At age thirty, my career blossomed and I bought my first house in a country club community called Saint Andrews. I had a young family at the time, and getting down to Florida on the weekends with my young family was impossible. I had to pick them up at school and then race to the airport to board a 7 p.m. flight, land in Florida at 10 p.m., and put the them to bed. On Sunday night, it was the same thing in reverse. It made school on Monday a very tired experience for my young kids.

There was a company called NetJets that sold fractional shares of jets and provided all the services of pilots, planes, food, and maintenance. I entered this company's program and started using their planes to fly south with my kids two out of four weekends per month in the winter. It was great but complicated, because when a plane breaks it is different than when a boat breaks. My friend had an expression: "I can swim. I can't fly." If a boat has a mechanical problem, most of the time you could still use it. If a plane has a mechanical problem, there is no flying until the issue is repaired. When you used NetJets, you bought a share of a certain plane. In the beginning, I started with the smallest and cheapest aircraft, figuring I would try the program out and see where it took me. As I become more comfortable with the planes, I started to upgrade to several types and sizes of aircraft. Some of the aircraft were great; some were just maintenance headaches that were broken most of the time.

At the time, I was in a program for a plane called the Hawker 4000. Every time I got to the airports, the pilots were waiting to tell me there was a hold on the flight because the plane had an issue and could not fly. Now, I was paying an absolute fortune for the convenience of a private aircraft, but four out of ten flights could not take off because of mechanical issues. NetJets would send a recovery plane hours later, but that was too late for a weekend trip with the kids to take off and get them in bed in Florida at a reasonable time. Later, I found out the nickname for the Hawker 4000 was Hanger Queen because of all the mechanical issues with this aircraft.

After months of this, out of frustration I wrote a letter to the President of NetJets, Mr. Santulli, and I copied Warren Buffett in my letter. Why did I send a copy to Warren Buffett? Mr. Buffett's company, Berkshire Hathaway, had purchased NetJets as an investment. Not thinking much of it, I figured that if Mr. Buffett's staff or personal assistant read his mail, then someone would call Richard Santulli and more attention would be focused on the issues. I would get some sort of credit against my account or a more reliable aircraft.

I have written many letters in my life to owners or CEOs of companies and have never gotten a response from the person I wrote the letter to. Usually, some employee calls me back and tries to help me.

One day, I am sitting in my office watching the Gore vs. Bush presidential election results (when they were counting chads in a disputed election). My secretary buzzes me and says some old guy is on the phone claiming he is Warren Buffett. I am trying to think who might be playing a joke on me—not remembering that I had copied Warren Buffett on my letter to the president of NetJets the previous month.

My secretary puts the phone call through, and I answer it. To my utter shock, on the other end of the line a man says, "Mr. Cutler, this is Warren Buffett." For a moment, I am numb. I am talking to a legend, the richest man in the world.

I quickly say, "Mr. Buffett, it is an honor to speak to you, but I must tell you I am in complete shock. It is difficult to get the words out of my mouth." Warren Buffett, in a very folksy and calm way, says, "Mr. Cutler I am responding to your letter to Richard Santulli, my president of NetJets, about your problems. I noticed from your letterhead that you are the largest homebuilder in the Philadelphia market, and I love to talk to people about their businesses."

From that point on, little tiny David Cutler had a forty-five-minute conversation with the one of the greatest investment minds in the world. The entire conversation felt normal; it was fluid, fun, and easy going with zero-intimidation of who I was talking to or what we covered in our forty-five minutes of conversation. I felt as though I was talking to a smart guy at a coffee shop about business and everything that was happening in the world, including the crazy, contested presidential election.

As we concluded our conversation, Mr. Buffett said he would investigate my issues and have someone report back to me as to how they would be resolved. He thanked me for my time (really, thanking me for my time!) and gave me his personal phone number stating that if I ever felt the need to talk to him to just call him on this phone.

After that conversion, every time I called NetJets to make a plane reservation, it was a much different experience. Maybe when the administer punched my name into the computer to make my reservation, bells and whistles went off and lights flashed on the computer (just kidding). My problems went from being a pain in the ass to only minor issues.

I learned so much from this interaction with Warren Buffett. First, this man was a sponge and a student. He sucked my brain dry about the NetJets company that he had invested in and gained valuable information that his executives would never tell him about from a customer.

He saw that I had the largest homebuilding footprint in the Philadelphia market and wanted to know all about my business: what I see in the future, what we did, how we built it, who bought houses from us, and on and on. Can you imagine Warren Buffett asking little Davey Cutler about the homebuilding business? All of this interrogation was done without even realizing it. I only understood the volume of information I had given up days later when I replayed our conversation in my head.

Now I know why this man is the most successful investor of all time. He listens, he digests, he asks, then he listens again. It does not matter who he is talking to—he is always the student. There's no ego, just a folksy way about him that charms the information and knowledge out of the forty-five minutes he spends with you. For the rest of my business career, when I engaged with someone, I always think about my conversation with Warren Buffett and how informative and instructional it was. He let you understand that he wants to learn from you, not lecture you.

Every year, Warren Buffett auctions off a lunch with him for charity held on the stock channel CNBC. For years I heard that this lunch went for $3 million, $4 million, or whatever cost. I always said to myself, "These people have way too much money, ego, and time to spend $4 million to have lunch with Warren Buffett." Now in retrospect, having spent a precious (free) forty-five minutes on the phone with this man, I understand why any titan of industry and or investing hedge fund giant would spend millions of dollars to have a one-on-one conversation with the greatest investor of all time and an amazing human being. I was lucky that I was on the receiving end of a once-in-a-lifetime experience.

CHAPTER 31
G.O.A.T: Greatest of All Time

There are two books that are must-reads. One is *Talking to G.O.A.T.s: The Moments You Remember and the Stories You Never Heard,* by Jim Gray; the other is *Wisdom from the Greatest CEO, Founders, and Game Changers,* by David Rubenstein.

The Jim Gray book is about the greatest athletes of all time. Jim was a sports commentator (a GOAT himself and twelve-time Emmy award winner) for most of his career, and he had the opportunity to become friendly with many of the greats in the sports world, such as Mohammad Ali, Michael Jordan, Kobe Bryant, Michael Phelps, Mike Tyson, LeBron James, and more. The book includes personal interviews that give an intimate insight to these great athletes, the best in their sport of all time. Jim examines how money, celebrity, the media, and power interact and how sports, more than any other institution, has led to momentous transformation in American society. What truly makes Jim's interviews with these GOATs are his insightful questions that carry a theme of the struggle, failure, and greatness brought out in all these athletes.

For example, when Muhammad Ali was drafted to fight in the Vietnam War, he lost his heavyweight title. Yet he came all the way back. When Michael Jordan's father was shot and killed while sleeping in his car at a rest stop, Jordan retired from basketball. After trying to play professional baseball, he ended up coming back after a few years to become more successful than ever. Michael Phelps fought suicide and depression for years; he overcame all that to become the greatest Olympic swimmer of all time. Mike Tyson needs no introduction of his struggles in life. From a childhood of crime, to the death of his mentor, to the heavyweight championship of the world, then jail and back to the heavyweight championship of the world. All of these G.O.A.T.s have one thing in common—beating unbelievable adversity and challenges with determination and victory.

Billionaire David Rubenstein is the co-founder of a private equity firm, the Carlyle Group, and he has an unbelievable business mind. He's also an author and the host of two television shows, where he interviews some of the greatest businesspeople of all time. I was introduced to David Rubenstein after reading his book *How to Lead: Wisdom from the World's Greatest CEOs, Founders, and Game Changers.* The book includes interviews with Bill Gates, Jeff Bezos, Ruth Bader Ginsburg, Warren Buffett, Oprah Winfrey, and many more visionaries about their lives and careers. These are people who changed our world in many ways—how we think, shop, function, and survive—and it shows how they manage the decision-making process, success and failure, innovation and change, and crisis management.

These are the GOATs of the business world. Their interviews and stories will give you insight into the motivation, determination, and will it takes to lead a company and be a game changer in the world. For example, the book profiles Oprah Winfrey, an African American woman who has built a giant business in a world largely controlled by white men. She is a billionaire who overcame the personal struggles of her childhood abuse and body image, inspiring millions of people to journey into a new world—a world that is different from what they are used to or have seen before.

The stories in both books are funny, motivational, brilliant, head-scratching, and life altering. There are many people in this world who have lived incredible lives, and it is truly fun to have a ringside seat in their adventures.

CHAPTER 32

The Art of Aging Gracefully

One thing is certain: You are going to age and eventually die. The art of aging gracefully has been studied over the years with some success. We all want to look young for as long as possible, but then there is too much. Some people, especially women, pile on the plastic surgery. First, they get their eyes done, but of course that has an impact on the rest of their face. Then they start messing around with their neck, their ears, their nose, and then of course it's time for the full facelift. I have had a front-row seat to plastic surgery, both good and bad. The trick is to look as natural as possible with smooth lines, but not too much that you look like a freak.

One night, I was out at a bar with my friend Tom. There was a woman at the bar who must have had her lips injected (why, I do not know); her lips were twice the size of normal lips, and they looked almost freakish. Tom sat on one side of her, and I sat on the other. We started to laugh and joke around with her until we got to the point of asking her about her lips. She claimed they were natural (which they were not, but anyway) and I challenged her to "make out" with Tom to prove they were real. She agreed, and the two of them went at it with a passionate kiss right at the bar! After about two minutes, Tom proclaimed that her lips felt amazing, but they couldn't be real because they felt too good!

Today, there are even posterior (butt) implants and tummy tucks, but the most popular surgery for women is a breast augmentation (or a boob job, as it is commonly referred to in the industry). Over the years, I have seen good boob jobs, bad boob jobs, soft boob jobs, hard boob jobs, and large boob jobs. You might say I am an expert in this area, because 98% of the women I have dated have had a boob job. For the women I have dated and spoken to, this was a self-motivated factor for them; they were extremely excited after finally deciding to get breast augmentation surgery. Over the years, our bodies start to succumb to gravity. A boob job is one way to stop gravity in its tracks and restore a chest to its former glory (or better). This can be a huge boost to confidence, and I would highly recommend it, if you can afford the process.

Plastic surgery is not mutually exclusive to women. Men also enjoy the motivational effects of looking good. Of course, men get nose jobs, eye jobs, face lifts, chin, or turkey-neck repairs. The most popular plastic surgery for men is the hair transplants. (Men are completely obsessed with their hair and hair loss.) While there have been many remedies for hair loss, none are as effective as good old hair plugs. The process is expensive and painful, but the result is terrific, at least judging by the celebrities that I have seen such as John Travolta. Elon Musk, Donny Wahlberg, Sylvester Stallone, and others.

One of the best ways to improve your appearance, for both men and women, is getting your teeth redone or capped, wearing braces, or even doing something as simple as whitening. Your smile is important, and good dental care creates a world of difference in an individual's confidence. If you have rotten teeth, then that can be a turn off. Someone who has good teeth is immediately perceived as attractive because of their smile. Work on your dental appearance and health. It is easily accessible to most of the public with a wide range of choices and prices.

Looking good is a huge motivation in life, but it can be a daily grind. Everyone at one point or another has been on a diet or worked out at a gym. But they often treat it as a temporary solution to a lifelong problem. People lose the weight; they look and feel great. Then because food is delicious and eating is fun, they put the weight back on. The weight gain makes them lose their motivation and energy and they become get depressed.

Obesity can creep up on you. You gain five pounds one year, and that doesn't seem so much. But at five pounds per year, over ten years, you will have gained fifty pounds. This is not good. Stay true to yourself. If you stay on course and exert some control, it is not too hard to snap back into shape by losing ten pounds. But if you let yourself go too far, it becomes a huge undertaking to drop thirty or forty pounds, and it may feel frustrating and depressing. Stay out of that zone.

I was overweight my entire life, and it was difficult. I love to wear nice clothes, but it is frustrating when you are overweight. I have tried so many fad diets over the years that it became somewhat of a joke. This past year, my college-age son convinced me to become a vegetarian. I said to myself, "What can I eat all day?" Guess what? There is a lot to eat! I do not eat meat chicken, or diary, and only occasionally will I eat a little fish. What I like about this diet is that I can eat all the carbs I want, and I can drink clear alcohol (in my case, that's tequila).

In four months, I have lost twenty-two pounds. I have never felt or looked better. I do not understand the process of why this happened, but the results are clear. I no longer feel starved all day, as I did with traditional diets. It was my birthday recently, and I took myself and all my kids out to a great steak house in the city. It was the first time in six months that I had a bite of steak. It was delicious, but did I really miss it? The answer is no. When the steak entered my mouth. it tasted great for about twenty seconds, but after one hour I felt bloated. It was certainly not worth the twenty seconds per bite of enjoyment. Eating should be entertaining with the goal of feeling satisfied. The byproduct is feeling full and looking good. Fitting into all of your clothes and feeling good outweighs the twenty seconds of pleasure per bite, and that's true of the any of the foods that are not good for you. If you eat a delicious desert, the enjoyment of tasting it lasts one minute. The effect on your body lasts hours or a full day. Is that one minute of enjoyment worth it?

For forty years, I wore a suit and tie to work every day. It was amazing to get dressed every day and feel—and look—good. Former President George W. Bush used to wear a suit and tie to the Oval Office, saying, "This office is a serious place, and you must dress seriously to be in it." George W. Bush claims that he never was in the Oval Office without his suit jacket on. That is serious. No one says that wearing a suit and tie is paramount to happiness. Wear what you feel good in and that makes you happy when put it on. It puts you in a great mood when you look in the mirror at the start of the day and are happy with your outfit and appearance. As you age, the clothes you wear can help make you feel young and hip. Clothes can help the aging process feel better and become more enjoyable.

It's important to age gracefully and put your best foot forward, both for yourself and for your mental health. If your looks or your age get you down, there's nothing wrong with plastic surgery, if you can afford it. It can make you feel great. If losing your hair is a big item on your list, then get hair transplants to boost your self-esteem.

If your smile is poor, then get it fixed. Start simple with things like getting yourself in shape. Once you lose weight and get in shape, all of the other enhancements will fall into place, including your self-esteem and self-respect.

Do not give up on yourself. Keep plugging away and continue to look and feel your best.

CHAPTER 33

A Lesson in Simple Adversity

In my office, I have the TV tuned to CNBC, otherwise known as the stock channel, all day long. Every so often, there is an advertisement for the Wounded Warriors. One after the other, veterans appear on the TV, many without arms or legs, other their face shot up. The commercial asks for a few pennies a month to help these wounded warriors or their families get a house of their own. Each wounded warrior sits there and says that he does not regret what he did or the fact that he lost a limb, and he would be happy to go back and fight again. Can you imagine losing an arm or a leg, living with that loss, and then making a statement that you would go back and fight again! Their sacrifice was worth it.

When I travel, I often see families with children who have special needs. Many of their parents give the bulk of their lives, and so much of their love, to raise children under these challenging circumstances. The care, time, and expense needed to give a special-needs child a good life is motivational.

For years, I participated in the Children's Hospital of Philadelphia, or CHOP. Our company sponsored their Carousel Ball, a big year-end event that celebrated the doctors and companies instrumental in helping this hospital. The hospital wanted me on the board, but I felt I could be more productive being affiliated with the hospital than as a

A Lesson in Simple Adversity

working board member. My wife at the time sat on the board instead of me. She was very qualified and proved a big asset to the hospital. At that time, CHOP was the number-one children's hospital in America in terms of care and research. This was very impressive for the city of Philadelphia.

I used to receive many calls from friends and families who had a problem with a child or a grandchild. They would seek my assistance in getting their child or grandchild into the hospital for care. I would always do what I could, no matter who they were, to see that the child received the best care possible immediately.

The truth is that you are not one of the best children's hospitals in America because you are lucky. The reason you exist is people and money. You need to raise large amounts of money to support the research and build the fabulous facilities needed to grow and build on that success. It is like a college football team. The great colleges get the great coaches and players and thus continue to be great. The same is true for hospitals. The great hospitals get great doctors, administrators, and of course huge endowments.

Whenever someone asked for help, I never said, "You need to donate." Long after the child was returned to health, I would call and ask them to come down to the hospital to see what CHOP was about. When I walk someone through the halls of this hospital, we would come upon room after room of kids. One kid, who was only one-week old, had just had open-heart surgery on a heart the size of a peanut. We would enter the oncology unit and see bald children who had been there for 436 days (you could tell by the sign on their door) in cancer treatment. We would stand outside a neonatal unit where there might be a child who weighed only two or three pounds. This amazing hospital fixes children. Unfortunately, not all of them

David Cutler

get fixed (there is a reason it is called practicing medicine), but the majority of the children do.

I got involved in the hospital when my now thirty-five-year-old son had a cancerous growth on the side of his head. For CHOP, this was routine, but I was impressed by how everything was overseen. I said to myself, "Life is so good for me. I need to give back." All of the doctors and nurses wear colorful hospital scrubs and the areas for children are fun and vibrant. Before a child starts his or her procedure, the hospital gives the child what they call "giggle juice." Before you know it, the child is asleep and on his way to get fixed!

Years later, my third child had phenomena in his lung and was admitted to CHOP. This was serious; his had lung collapsed and they had to re-inflate it through three or four puncture marks in front and back. I will never forget the first night I spent sleeping on the sofa in his room; I could hear the helicopters landing on the roof at all hours of the night and into the morning. I kept thinking to myself, "My son is fine. He has a few holes in his chest, but he did not need a helicopter to get here." The helicopters landing on the roof brought kids who were in serious trouble, but they were lucky they were at a serious place. Here, they were safe and cared for.

Associated with CHOP is a place called the Ronald McDonald House. It is a special place on the hospital campus where families who cannot afford hotel rooms for the weeks or months while their kids are getting treatment. This became one of my favorite places to go whenever the world had gotten me down. I would go in there, day or night, just to be with the families and the children who were being taken care of at the hospital. These were folks trying to live a normal life while their children were dealing with serious illnesses. Watching

A Lesson in Simple Adversity

people make the best of a horrible situation changes your perspective; it makes the problems in your life feel minor.

For my fiftieth birthday, my mother gave me the most incredible gift I have ever received. It was a weekly Wednesday night appointment with a clown called Judy Trudy at the Ronald McDonalds House, and it was good for one year. Judy Trudy would show up at the Ronald McDonald House with blow-up balloons to make dogs or hats or whatever she could out of those balloons to make the sick kids smile and laugh while they tried to survive. After the year was over, I paid for Judy Trudy to show up every Wednesday to continue the love and care these children needed.

This chapter is simply about adversity. If you are lucky, if you are not suffering, then you should count your blessings. People fight adversity all day, every day of their lives. Sure, we might complain when the grass is dead on the front lawn, or if we have a lousy meal at a restaurant, or even if our car breaks down and gets a flat tire. But think about the alternative, such as the people who are fighting for their lives—for their existence—and who have a very rough life where we are so fortunate. If you spend the weekend at the beach and it rains the whole time, is that really adversity or the worst thing ever? The answer is that it is not. When we look at others who are truly having a challenging time, it measures what you can do to live an improved life because you are truly blessed. The energy that you would expend overcoming adversity can be spent moving forward in a positive direction. Just like the wounded warriors who say they would do it all over again without missing a beat. They were proud to serve their country and will rise again to be strong. These sick kids will get stronger because of what they have been through.

Adversity is difficult, but when you rise above it you are stronger. You understand that we are truly blessed, that our problems are not real problems that can slow us down from moving forward. One of the most rewarding lessons in this book is this. If you are truly blessed, financially and physically, you have a chance to give back. There are wonderful places that exist because of the people who support them. To give anything is very rewarding, to both you and any cause that you are support.

CHAPTER 34

Stucco Nightmare: The Toughest Challenge of My Career

In 2000, our building competition started to use stucco instead of vinyl siding. Since we were the largest builder in the marketplace, with over twenty-five communities under construction, to stay competitive we had to use stucco on the sides and rear of a home instead of vinyl siding. The process of switching to stucco was not easy. It requires our firm to redraw all our plans and specifications, as well as seek all new approvals from the various townships and municipalities. In addition, we were in Philadelphia where it is 100 degrees in the summer and 10 degrees in the winter. Applying stucco in this climate was a challenge to say the least, because you could not do this application in the winter only when the temperature was above freezing. But stucco was now the trend, and we could not be competitive unless we used the stucco product, so we started to build our homes with stucco. Even worse, each year that we used the stucco product, the townships changed the application process so we had to relearn and reengineer our plans every year on the application of stucco to our homes. Putting up vinyl siding was easier; it came in a box, and you nailed it up in a day. But we were stuck with stucco.

From 2000 to 2008, we built about 1,000 stucco homes out of the 16,000 built over our company history. As time went on, the homeowners started to incur problems with their stucco homes. The issue was simple: Wood expands and contracts. Stucco is concrete and does not move, let alone expand and contract. A house expands and contracts over the seasons, but the stucco cracks because it does not move. When the stucco cracks in the winter, it only compounds the issue, because water or snow gets into the cracks and expands and contracts and creates a big mess. Now the stucco is compromised; water finds its way through these cracks behind the stucco with no way out. The water moistens the wood framing, which causes mold to form on the wood. In Florida and in the south, stucco is applied to concrete blocks that do not expand and contract. As a result, the concrete block wall does not move, and the stucco does not crack or freeze. There are several other theories of how the water penetrates the home, from framing, roofing, and everything in between.

It takes several winters for stucco to crack, and this allows water to enter the framing of a home. Once water enters behind the stucco, it will start to show up in the framing and in the wall cavity of the home and you will start to see spots on your drywall.

To further compound these issues, many of the recommended window applications are universal; they are not designed for the north where the house was made of wood and would expand and contract, causing the seals on the windows to start to break apart and leaking water to find its way behind the stucco.

Finally, before the stucco was applied years ago, we used to use black tar paper that allowed the wall to breathe. With new building products, we now use a product called Tyvek wrap. Tyvek is like plastic; it does not allow the walls to breathe. If water penetrates behind the Tyvek wrap, it stays there and never dries out, causing the wood framing to stay wet and eventually rot.

In addition, the state of Pennsylvania incorporated Act 222, which sealed the house so tightly that no chilly air would infiltrate into the home. This created problems because a home needs to be able to breathe. With no ventilation in or out of a home, any moisture that was trapped behind the walls could cause mold.

All of these building changes were done after the plans were approved by the townships and under the watchful eye of the township building inspector, who would inspect any given home over twenty times from start to finish. If at any time any of these building inspectors were not happy with the construction of the home, they would stop all construction until whatever deficiencies that were found were corrected.

As time went on, the stucco problems for not only our company but all homebuilders in the northeast started to surface and grew larger and larger. At the beginning of this process, we sent service crews out to homes to caulk and remove windows or repair cracks in the stucco due to complaints. Each passing year, the townships changed the requirements of how to apply stucco in our geographic area due to complaints from homeowners who had stucco homes.

By 2008, with all the new requirements to apply stucco, the additional costs, and the downtime caused by not being able to work with concrete in the freezing winter, all of the builders decided to switch back to vinyl siding. Ironically, the buying public seemed to like this product more! It was maintenance free and easy to apply the product in the dead of a freezing-cold winter. Plus, you could stay on a better timeline to deliver the new home to the buyers. Throughout the northeast, as people started to experience issues with stucco, the competitive landscape of other builders switched from stucco into other products.

Stucco Nightmare: The Toughest Challenge of My Career

Around 2010, the lawsuits started to come in from a multitude of lawyers who represented homeowner claims of stucco leakage on their homes. At this point, we had stopped building stucco homes for competitive reasons, as well as due to the complexity of all the yearly township code changes. The fact that we were not building stucco homes anymore did not stop the lawyers from the previous stucco houses we had built from filing hundreds of cases against our firm. Our firm was just one of many national and local builders in our market who had built stucco homes with the same codes, applications, and contractors and who were being inundated with stucco lawsuits. If you were a homebuilder in the northeast and you used stucco between the years 2000 and 2008, you were being sued.

Our firm spent tens of millions of dollars repairing homes or paying for homes to be repaired, as well as paying the cost of litigation trying to get our arms around the stucco issues. Our firm had a huge amount of insurance that we paid millions and millions of dollars for in premiums over the years and that should have covered all the stucco repairs. After fixing and defending the stucco cases, with some help from the insurance companies through 2016, the insurance companies now decided to sue our firm to get out of paying for repairs. Why would the insurance companies do this you ask? Simple: Because they could. The insurance companies were multi-billion-dollar corporations; they knew that the homebuilders could not afford the huge onslaught of litigation. The insurance companies threw big-time lawyers at us to try and avoid paying the stucco claims. That is their game: Stall, delay, and deny. As the stucco cases went to trial, I can honestly say we did not win one case. The homeowners sued based upon three facts: manufacture recommendations for installing windows, industry standards for applying stucco, and local township building codes. We quickly learned that we could not serve all three masters and that the cases were not winnable. The building inspector was the boss of all bosses; you needed to satisfy him, or you could not move forward.

Here's a hypothetical example. If the building inspector wanted you to put twenty nails in a window in order to install the window in the wall, and the manufacturer of that window only wanted ten nails, then you would lose in court. We had to do what the building inspector wanted, and if that was twenty nails, then the window manufacture held that they were not liable because we did not follow their recommendations. They would claim that that was why the window leaked. Since building inspectors cannot be held accountable for their decisions by the courts, we were on the hook.

There were many different manufacturer recommendations for stucco application by all of the various stucco companies. Again, we followed what the local building codes were for applying stucco. Again, the local codes were in stark contrast to what was the industry standard for applying stucco because each application of stucco was different in different geographic areas and different temperatures. Again, when going into court, the stucco lawyers would point this out as the reason why there were problems with the stucco. Again, we had to build exactly the way the building inspectors required us to build. When a house is completed and going to settlement, you receive a certificate of occupancy that says that the home complies with all township rules, regulations, and standards. Unfortunately, the local codes may not match with industry standards.

As we continued forward, our insurance companies fought us every step of the way until one day we were in court for a case involving multiple homeowners. Our building company, the one that had built these houses, had no assets, so we were relying on the insurance companies to pay the claims. The only assets in the company were the insurance policies. The judge in the case suggested that since the building companies had all these lawsuits and no assets, it would be prudent to file for bankruptcy and let the Federal Bankruptcy Trustee deal with the insurance companies rather than our firm. The judge, in his wisdom, felt that the insurance companies would have a much different level of respect for a Bankruptcy Trustee and a judge than us, disavowing coverage against the stucco claims.

Prior to this court date, the building company engaged in hundreds of lawsuits involving stucco. It is safe to assume that the bulk of our time was consumed with the litigation involving these three hundred stucco homes. There was a point in this litigation where I was in court daily. The sheriffs at the front door of the courthouse would greet me with a big hello and let me walk around the metal detectors because they saw me so often. At this point, it made sense to take the judge's advice and file for bankruptcy in that building company. This would suspend the ongoing litigation and allow the bankruptcy trustee to deal with the insurance companies; they would try and create a fund that would satisfy the stucco lawyers and their clients.

After four years, the bankruptcy trustee was finally able to make a deal with the insurance companies and the stucco lawyers to settle the claims. The insurance companies, exhausted from the litigation, as well as the stucco lawyers reached a financial settlement in the millions of dollars. The bankruptcy actions suspended the litigation and allowed the trustee, the insurance companies, the stucco lawyers, and the bankruptcy judge to reach a financial settlement.

In authoring this book about business and life through my involvement in all this litigation and dealing with stucco, I had to make very tough decisions where the option is bad or bad. In the

16,000 homes that we built over forty years, we had two lawsuits total that did not involve stucco. One was a nine-year-old house that had a dishwasher overflow. The other lawsuit was over a retired wrestler who threw himself down a flight of stairs in a house under construction so he could injure himself. Then he could sue us for not having signage up that stated there was no trespassing because the house was under construction. That was it. Then stucco came along, and all hell broke loose.

This was the difficulty of the problem as I saw it: How to figure a way out of this mess and settle with the insurance companies and stucco plaintiffs. In all this massive litigation, all we had were lawyers. None of these lawyers had a global view of things. Some dealt with court trials, business, and marketing throughout the process; there were also insurance companies, townships and building inspectors, and many other facets of this massive litigation. What we needed was a conductor—an individual who had a huge business background and who dealt with massive litigation. This individual could have run this litigation problem like a business, with areas they would control (much like the CEO of a business) rather than having a bunch of lawyers running around in all directions reacting to emergencies. There was no one lawyer who oversaw the entire ball of wax, as they say. I personally had no experience in court or in being a lawyer, so I relied heavily on what was represented to me rather than directing the flow of information and problem-solving in the most efficient manner.

Having now gone through this unfortunate experience, I think that if someone were to hire me as a consultant on a case involving a massive disruption, I now have the set of tools and the chops to work things out in the most efficient manner. The most important thing is to identify the problem and try and assess how big the issues are. If you can understand with reasonable certainty the size of the issue,

Stucco Nightmare: The Toughest Challenge of My Career

then you can form a game plan to address the size and scope of the problem and the solution.

At the very beginning, you need to hire a lead lawyer who will manage all of the other different lawyers. (Please remember, there are many lawyers involved.) Some lawyers are hired by the insurance companies, some are hired by the subcontractors, others are hired by the window manufactures, and even more are hired by the mortgage companies. All of these lawyers have separate agendas, and they do not work as a team. The only time they worked as a team was when the bankruptcy trustee took over.

This had to be the most difficult experience of my business career.

CHAPTER 35

How Do You Eat an Elephant?

There is an old expression: "How do you eat an elephant?" The answer: "One bite at a time."

In business and in life, you will have problems that are difficult to resolve. When problem-solving, you need to look at the totality of the issues and produce a game plan that you can implement. I believe in the adage that you need to attack a bigger problem "one bite at a time." Trying to resolve all of the issues at once only dilutes each segment of the problem. You end up not getting anywhere because you are making only a little progress on solving a much bigger problem.

For example, take the stucco nightmare in the previous chapter. We obviously went about this the wrong way, because it cost a fortune and took four years to resolve. If, at the very beginning, we understood the enormity of the problem and why it was a problem, we would have been better able to address the issues. It had become an industry-wide problem, rather than our own individual problem. Because our firm was the largest builder in the marketplace, more attention was drawn to us. Other builders had five homes going up in one area, or three homes going up in another. Our firm had large-scale communities of over 100 homes, all of which were stucco. When the stucco problems hit the northeast, all builders were impacted, but we were affected more than others due to the size of our company.

When we look at history and understanding how problems in the past were resolved, we can apply those important lessons to solving problems in the future. In our case, we should have focused on the insurance companies up front and had them create a fund for the stucco payments. Doing this would have eliminated the need for all the litigation. If we had understood the enormity of the problem and recognized that the only real asset of the company was the insurance policies, then we could have been proactive and filed for Chapter 7 bankruptcy on day one instead of day 1200. A Chapter 7 bankruptcy says to the public: There are no assets and there is no reason to try and continue this entity moving forward. Many companies go through Chapter 11 bankruptcy, which is a reorganization plan. In our case, there was nothing to reorganize; Chapter 7 was the appropriate way to file. Our issue was that we should have done that on day one rather than wait four years, spend millions of dollars in litigation, and give one thousand hours fighting with the insurance companies. Yet none of the experts we hired advised us to file for Chapter 7 right away. Was the problem resolved anyway? Yes, but if we had approached it with the end in mind, it could have been resolved quicker.

When our firm attacked this problem, we tried to fix every issue rather than taking on each issue "one bite at a time." We could have looked to the insurance companies to find the cleanest way to go after the insurance companies and get them to the table on day one to resolve all the cases. After talking to the [many] lawyers, no one had suggested this as a viable, quick resolution. The lawyers wanted to defend every action and fight the insurance companies. Other than the insurance companies, there was no one to go after to help pay the claims! Lawyers make money by being lawyers. Insurance companies make money by collecting premiums; when it is time to pay, they will delay and stall until the court steps in.

Taking things "one bite at a time" would have meant immediately going into Chapter 7 bankruptcy as the cases started to roll in, suspending all future litigation and forcing the insurance companies to settle the cases through the federal bankruptcy judge and the bankruptcy trustee. If I could have found a businessperson who was in the business of crisis management, then this is how he would have resolved things. I am now an expert in crisis management. If ever asked, I could certainly show any company a path forward about who to talk to and how to proceed.

The "one bite at a time" adage applies to everything in life, whether it is planning a wedding, starting a business, buying a house, or even selecting a college to attend. While you need a global game plan of what to do, once you get into the details of the project, you need to do things "one bite at a time" to finally reach the finish line.

Let's say you want to buy a house. First, you need to decide how much you can afford to pay. A nicer home in a less desirable area might give you more "bang for your buck." For example, I lived on one street throughout the entire time I was in the Hamptons in New York. Now, you either lived on the north side or the south side of that street. The south side of the street was considered very desirable, while the north side was not as desirable. I never understood why. It was a friggin' road! On the north side of the street, you could buy three times the house than on the south side of the street. The two were one minute apart. There were beautiful homes on both sides of the street. But one side had huge snob appeal; the other was more farm-like. As far as the resale value, the two sides of the street were the same. All boats rise at the same time. If things are good, then all of the houses on both sides of the street will increase in value; if things are lousy, then all of the houses will decrease in value.

Once you decide how much you can afford, then you can start to look in areas where you want to live in. Examine your range of options. You might want to live in the next town over to get a better bang for your buck or purchase a lesser home in a fancier area. If school districts are important to you (if your child is not going to a private school), then you might have to settle on less of a house to get in a better school district or a better house in a less desirable school district.

After you establish those options, then you can start to look at houses and weigh the tradeoffs: new versus old, more bedrooms versus fewer, big yard but less of a house, small yard but more of a house. Finally, you can decide on a house given all the options that are available to you.

The simplicity of buying a home is more complicated than the three steps laid out here, but it serves a basic understanding of the process: "one bite at a time." Work your way down the list of available options until you make a final decision.

As you go through life, you can apply the adage of "one bite at a time" to everything you do. At the end of the process, you will hopefully come to the best conclusion and outcome.

CHAPTER 36
Failure Is Winning

Very few people go through life without experiencing failure. Trust me, no one wants to fail. It feels awful, and the process is mind-numbing. Failure at every level is excruciating. Failure as a parent, failure at a relationship, failure in business, failure as a son, daughter, or friend. Pick a noun, and you can add the word failure next to it for almost everyone.

Here's the trick: Treat failure as winning. Take something from that experience and learn how you dealt with it and eventually overcame it. As Mike Tyson used to say, "Everyone has a plan, until they get punched in the mouth." This is life, failure will occur, and it will suck. The trick is to understand why you failed and not to blame anyone else. Rationalize it as if it were to occur again and consider how you could manage things differently, if possible. There are some situations where the options are bad or...bad. If that is the situation, then take the bad and get the hell out!

Failure is winning. It is how you deal with failure that allows you to win. There is no law in any state that says you must make money or that every deal is a winner. Sometimes you get involved in a situation, either business-related or personal, that is just a bad deal. Ask any group of businesspeople, and they will all tell you that, in their lengthy

Failure Is Winning

business careers, they have had at least one failure or more. Failure teaches you not make the same mistake again.

There are many degrees of failure, and people view failure differently. In business, someone may view failure as not making as much money as they thought they should in a given year. Others may view failure much more dramatically, such as in declaring bankruptcy. In my case, the option of bankrupting a company was always distasteful. In the end, it was the only way all parties involved could focus on a higher authority. It was an exceedingly difficult experience, but one I now understand. Either way, it is the experience that you need to learn from and then move on or move up.

Let's assume you are in business, and you are not making as much as you think you could or should. Obviously, you'll try other things to increase your profit margin, but there is always a defining point where you must value your time. If you feel that you have exhausted all options, then it may be time to take a fresh look at the business and possibly consider selling it or taking the time to do something else. You can view this as a failure, but I view it as a valuable experience.

There is an expression that many wounded warriors say after recovering from injury: "If I had not failed, it would not feel so good now." What does that mean? These veterans are living with a life-altering injury; they did not think they were going to survive the accident, let alone the rehab required to rebuild their life. There are wonderful organizations that buy or build handicap-accessible homes for these wounded warriors. Now that they can live on their own and rebuild their lives, they learn to appreciate everything so much more. They see it through a much different lens.

When you listen to interviews with these wounded veterans, you'll hear them say that they would not change a thing about their life or experience; they accept the consequences of their situation. They do not look at what happened as failure but as another chapter in their life—one with consequences that made them stronger and taught them they will overcome any obstacles.

I have a friend who I went to high school with that is a remarkable guy. He is six-feet, one-inch tall and weighs over four hundred pounds and has had a very rough life. We grew up middle class in a nice suburban neighborhood and attended public high school together. Our class held about seven hundred kids. My friend was in my brother's class, two years behind mine. After high school, most of us went on to college, and after finishing college we went on to some sort of career, usually the career as what their parents did for a living.

My friend, let's call him Jack, graduated from college and did something different. Jack started at a penny stock brokerage firm trading stock. Within a year, he was making over one million dollars annually and was one of the top producers at the firm. It was incredible! Then something happened mechanically in the firm, and he was thrown out and his license was taken away. A million-dollar-a-year job at age twenty-four, and it was gone. He had failed.

Jack moved on to the cell phone business and within six months was the number-one writer of new accounts in the state of Florida where he now lived. As he moved up in both industries, he became addicted to cocaine. I used to say to him, "How can you weigh almost four hundred pounds and be addicted to cocaine?" His response was that it just made him eat food faster. Something happened in his cell phone business, and he was again banished from the industry and lost his job. Then something really bad happened: He was arrested for selling drugs. Jack retained a great lawyer and only spent (what he says) were the worst seventeen days of his life in jail.

Failure Is Winning

When Jack got out of jail, he went to a rehab center and became sober. So, what did Jack do next? Well, he became the number-one teacher and coach in rehab centers in the area. After a period of giving back and helping others, Jack needed more money, so he left that business and went into the flea market selling sneakers. Guess what? Jack had the largest-volume business at the flea market and sold the most product of anyone else. However, standing on his feet all day was extremely hard because of Jack's weight, so he got out of the flea market business. He sold his position to someone else, but not before proving to himself and everyone else he could be number one.

Then tragedy struck. Jack's twenty-two-year-old daughter was in a car accident. An off-duty police officer with four other people in the cab of his truck blew through a stop sign at a high speed and smashed the side of the car Jack's daughter was in. She was injured and partially paralyzed. Four years later, she is still in rehab. She will be a challenge the rest of her life. The police who responded to the scene allowed the off-duty officer who hit her to remain roadside for six hours prior to administering a DUI test.

For the next few years, Jack worked part-time and spent the bulk of his time taking his daughter to rehab and helping her adjust to her new life. While doing this, Jack got back into the cell phone business, and you guessed it, is the number-one seller of cell phone accessories in the South Florida market. At this point, "number-one" is his middle name.

This is an incredible story of a human being. Every time Jack failed, he dusted himself off, got up, and rebuilt his life. Today, Jack is seventeen years sober and helps motivate people with his struggles, failures, and successes. You can find him, most nights, sitting at the local cigar bar enjoying a smoke and hanging around other, telling them the tales of life.

For Jack, failure was winning. He would have never known what winning was unless he had first experienced failure. Most of the people you meet have lived a normal, uneventful life; then you meet a wounded warrior, someone who has dealt with failure in a big way—like Jack—or with something as personal as a divorce after many years of marriage and raising children. It is these experiences that make you appreciate what you have and how you should look at life.

It's funny. I have a brother-in-law who has had a front-row seat to my adventures. He has a favorite expression: "My life is boring, and I love it."

CHAPTER 37

One More Chapter

I believe that, no matter how old you, whether personal or professional, there is one more chapter in your life.

In 2000, I had a summer home at the beach. Several houses away was the most magnificent home owned by a billionaire businessperson. It was architecturally beautiful, set on three beachfront lots that made it a perfect shore home. Over the years, while walking the streets or watching my kids ride their bikes, I would run into this neighbor. I always made small talk, and over the years that we both lived on that street we became friendly. He was older, and I was a kid who had caught a couple of breaks. He enjoyed talking to me and sharing the lessons from his life. I was a good listener and not a talker. So many people love to hear themselves talk but never listen. That's a huge mistake—always listen. You can't learn anything from only talking. If you listen to anyone, you can learn things that you did not know and can use later in life.

Anyway, one day I was talking to this neighbor and I said, "If you ever want to sell your house, I would love to buy it from you." He chuckled and told me that he also had a house in Maine. He primarily used this place when his kids and grandkids were around because it was easier to get to from Philadelphia rather than traveling to Maine. But he would always keep me in mind.

One More Chapter

Later, one of those TV shows (like TMZ) decided to pick on this neighbor because he was in the health care field. They decided to plant TV cameras in front of this home for a few weekends and do their exposé about the health care business. Now, this was a tough, a no-nonsense guy, and he hired lawyers to sue the TV show. That was "Part One" of his plan. "Part Two" was to get the hell out of this shore town. His main property was an imposing home in the Philadelphia suburbs set on forty to fifty acres with a long driveway, a gated entrance, and tons of landscaping. His house was set so far back from the street and had so much landscaping in front of it that it blocked all views; you could not see it from the street. There was no way that this TV show could get any footage of him, his family, and or his house. However, the shore was a different story. Here, his magnificent home was on the beach with other homes lining the shore. All of these homes fronted on a main street that was fifty feet away from his front door. There was no privacy, and any TV outlet could stand on the public street and film away, which is exactly what they did.

I had always been nice to this neighbor. Even though my ego was bursting with success as I started to make good money, I always listened and respected him. Even if I could get into some type of competitive conversation, I did not think that was appropriate.

Guess it was the right thing to do. One day my phone rings, and it is my neighbor. He goes on and on about this TV show, about the lack of privacy at this summer home and how could they photograph his house and his kids. Now that he has his own jet, he is going to sell this home and move to his Maine property. The jet was necessary to transport his family to Maine or Florida, where he would be able to get the privacy he so often sought.

We got right into it. I said, "What would you like for your home?" He stated his price of $7 million furnished and that it was non-negotiable. Now, when a billionaire says something is non-negotiable, he will hold to it until he gets his price met. He feels that the price is fair, and you know that he is not kidding around. Nothing at this shore town ever sold anywhere near that number, but at the same time, the house sat on three beachfront lots. It would cost a fortune to replicate. I figured that I could always tear the house down if I had to and sell the beachfront lots for what I had paid for the package. The realty was that the raw earth was worth more than the house. I agreed to buy the house, and we quickly settled. I was living three houses away in a much smaller home on the beach, so I had to sell my house first before I could purchase this new place. I put my house up for sale and, lucky for me, sold it immediately.

My wife at the time and I were still together, but things were bad, and it looked like I was headed for my second divorce. Either way, I was legally protected, so I went through with purchasing this house. After I had signed the sale agreement, we went over to walk through the property. My wife hated the gorgeous modern furniture and refused to move in! I was trying my best to keep my marriage alive, so this was just a new problem that I had created.

Regrettably, I called my neighbor and, feeling terrible, told him the story while he listened. I said, "I do not want or expect a reduction in the sale price, but I feel horrible that I cannot use the furniture." I asked if his kids or someone else could use the furniture because I would have to get rid of it if I want to stay married. He wasn't mad. In fact, he was extremely gracious and said he would take care of removing the furniture by the closing date.

Fast-forward to the settlement for the property. I was there with the owner's representative. They handed me the settlement sheet, and I see a credit for $500,000 for the furniture that he removed. I quickly told his lawyer that this must be a mistake, as I had agreed to pay the full price. The fact that my wife (by closing, we were no longer together) did not want or like the furniture was not his issue. His lawyer said that the owner appreciated my offer, but fair is fair. He wanted to give me the credit but would ask for a favor in the future. I said, "What favor?" The lawyer responded that he did not know but to expect a call. Wow! I was on the edge of my seat waiting for his call. In the meantime, I had the most magnificent house at the beach and an extra $500,000 in my pocket. I could wait with a big smile on my face.

Two months after the settlement of the house, I received a call from my neighbor. I thanked him for crediting the furniture and told him how pleased I was with the house. At that point, he told me that he needed some of the money back for a think-tank group that he was starting in Washington, DC called The Foundation for Defense for Democracies, a nonpartisan 501 research institute focusing on national security and foreign policy. He told me that it was a small group of remarkably successful businesspeople, and it would not require too much of my time during the year. Obviously, with the (credit for furniture) money in my pocket, I could not refuse. I happily agreed and sent my money to became a member of the board of The Foundation for Defense for Democracy. I was clearly the idiot in the room, but it was a fun experience.

In the meetings I attended, I learned a lot and met some interesting and successful businesspeople, many of whom were billionaires. One gentleman had founded one of the great retail businesses across America. One day I received a call from this gentleman, and he asked me for a favor. He lived in a country club community in South Florida where I had built about twenty-five homes. At the time, our concept was to buy an older home, tear it down, and build a bigger, newer, modern home. Only when the new home was done would we put it up for sale. (I did not want to be in the business of building homes for people from scratch.) This beautiful community in South Florida had started in the early 1980s and was completed by about 2004. The community was now over thirty years old. They were rebuilding and updating the clubhouse, golf courses, and amenities, such as the tennis courts. In this part of South Florida, they do not make any new ground, so the existing communities went through a transition, upgrading dramatically. Part of the upgrading process was people tearing down older homes down and building bigger, newer, more magnificent homes.

For purposes of this book, let's call this gentleman Bob. I returned Bob's call, and he asked if I would meet him at the community to see a lot he was thinking about buying to build a new home. Bob lived in an older home in the community and wanted to upgrade. I quickly agreed, and the next week I went out to the community to meet Bob at the lot he wanted to buy. I was simply giving him advice on the lot; I had no interest in building a custom home from scratch for him, as that was not my business.

The lot was magnificent and was one of the top five lots in the community. It was a double lot where you could build a large home and that backed up to a lake. I had to ask him a question though, before I gave him my opinion.

I said, "Bob, how old are you? Your career is over, and you are retired, although you participate in a lot of things."

Bob smiles and says, "I am eighty-eight years old."

I scratched my head and said, "You do realize that it will take two years to build a big new home? So that means you are moving in at age ninety."With another smile, he said, "Sure. That is correct. I am excited about it." So, I told him that, in my expert opinion, this is a gorgeous lot and he should go for it. The next day, he bought the lot and eventually built a gorgeous house. Bob is now ninety-five; he's in good health and in terrific shape and has enjoyed living in his home for the last five years. In his mind, he did not think or feel like he was eighty-eight, or even about being ninety once the house was done.

The point of the story is there is always one more chapter to life. Here was this phenomenally successful businessperson who, at eighty-eight years old, said to himself, "I want a new house." Then, he went out and built it. Bob had accomplished so much in his life to him this was a no brainer. He wanted one more chapter.

This brings me to the purpose of authoring this book. In my career, I have built 16,000 houses, 129 communities, and developed more than 20,000 building lots. I enjoyed that career, but with the difficulty of interest rates, economic cycles, supply-chain disruption, shortage of labor, banking difficulties, government oversight rules and regulations, and finally, all the litigation that exists in America, I decided that the building business was too difficult to continue at a grand scale. If you catch a great economic cycle, you can make a lot of money, but there are also the recession cycles where you can (and will) lose a ton of money if you get through them. It is like a game of musical chairs or blackjack: If you bet your big money on a bad hand, you can lose big.

I said to myself, "I have built 16,000 houses and had many difficulties and successes. I do not need the practice. Maybe I should try something else rather than do the same thing repeatedly, knowing there will be many challenges out of my control along the way.

As I finished my building career, I thought about what is next in my life. I decided as a form of therapy to write this book. I am fortunate to be a member of a golf club down in Florida. I am an early riser and have been my entire life. Another member of my golf club—James Patterson, the greatest author of all time—is also an exceedingly early riser. When I was out at the golf club early in the morning, I would see James, and we would always have a quick morning chat. James is a great guy, very friendly and generous with his time. He gave me some good advice. When I told him that I would like to write a motivation book about my career, he smiled and said, "Go for it. You might be surprised, and it could be a big success." Such a simple statement and hopefully great advice. I can tell you that, if nothing else comes out of this book (in terms of sales or success), writing it has been very therapeutic.

It is interesting that everything in life equates to "Left Foot, Right Foot," even the simplest tasks.

One weekend, I drove my car from Philadelphia to Florida, stopping along the way at Amelia Island to eat dinner and spend the night. The ride from Philadelphia to Amelia Island was twelve and a half hours. As I watched my GPS navigation on my phone, I could see the hours counting down: twelve hours to go, eleven hours to go. I listened to the radio, called my kids and then some friends: ten hours to go, nine hours to go. Suddenly, I was there. But it took putting one foot in front of the other to complete my mission. The same approach applies to going to the gym in the morning. Every day, I walk for forty-five minutes on the treadmill at various speeds. I watch the minutes like crazy, thinking how exhausted I am from drinking the night before, but I continue. In the three years that I have been working out, I have never stopped before the forty-five-minute mark. I watch the clock intently: ten minutes, then twenty minutes. Once I pass thirty minutes, I know I am home free. The rest is easy. It's just "left foot, right foot" until I get to where I am going. Then I am done, and I have won. I completed my mission of forty-five minutes on the treadmill. Then it's on to the next challenge of the day.

I was recently at my son's college graduation from a famous Ivy League school. The school has had many famous and successful graduates, yet the commencement speaker was just awful. Her career was mediocre and her message narcissistic. I was shocked that one of the top schools in the country, one that could have any alumni for the commencement, chose this person.

As I sat there and thought about the four days of festivities with my son, his frat buddies, and all the brilliant kids I interacted with, I felt that the school had let their graduates down on the biggest day of their lives. This speaker should have approached the microphone, told all the graduates to stand up give themselves a big round of applause, to hug the person next to them, and celebrate the next chapter in their life. I am sure many of these graduates had experienced countless nights spent studying, plus all of the problems and challenges of college life for the last four years. This was a graduation about life, and most importantly it was about them—what they hope for and can expect in the next chapter in life.

My "one more chapter" is this book. I hope it gives me an opportunity to speak to college graduates and to motivate them toward the greatness that lies in front of them. I promise to make them laugh, cry, and to celebrate their life. I hope it brings opportunities for motivational speaking engagements. I would love to talk to businesses and individuals about how they can move up to the next level in everything they do. And I hope that you have enjoyed the many stories that were part of my career and life, that you might receive some insights from the successes and failures of one person. Most of my career I listened and did not talk. Now, it is my turn to talk.